HOMING IN

a practical resource for religious education

First published in 1998 by Trentham Books Limited

Trentham Books Limited
Westview House
734 London Road
Oakhill
Stoke on Trent
Staffordshire
England ST4 5NP

British Cataloguing in Publication Data
A catalogue record for this book is available from the British Library
ISBN: 0 948080 87 6

Designed and typeset by Trentham Print Design and printed by
Cromwell Press Ltd, Wiltshire

HOMING IN

a practical resource for religious education

Angela Wood
with Jane Oxley – Lesley Prior – Pauline Sims
Illustrations Mike Kelly
Photographs Simon Potter

tb
Trentham Books

*For those with whom we share our homes
and those who have shared their homes with us*

Acknowledgements

Many individuals effectively became an 'extended family' to the project: it was born – and has matured – because of them: Martyn Cribb (former humanities adviser, Hounslow) saw the project's potential and gave it active support in the crucial early stages of 1989, while Sham Naib (former Inspector for multicultural education, Hounslow) endorsed its significance and lent it concrete assistance. Eluned Cole, Mary Donald and Rita James – teachers of infants in Hounslow – were involved in the project in its early phase and their practical suggestions shaped many of the artefacts and activities.

The late Ken Oldfield, when director of the BFSS National RE Centre, literally housed 'Homing In' – and hosted the 'Home Team' – from 1990 onwards when the project was being consolidated and disseminated more widely. It owes him an incomparable debt of gratitude for the warmth of his encouragement and the depth of his insights.

Simon Potter created an exciting visual record of the project by literally bending over backwards to take hundreds of photographs in the narrow confines of child-sized home corners! His work – some of which appears in this book – has been an invaluable resource for inservice training and display.

The line drawings which illustrate the artefacts – many of which serve as designs or templates – have all been produced by Mike Kelly whose artistic flair is matched by his attention to accuracy and authenticity.

Many of the artefacts paradoxically owe their simplicity of production to a complex process of design (often by trial and error!) in the developmental phase. Les Thompson cheerfully gave vital no-nonsense advice about the execution of some of the artefacts.

'Homing In' courses have been run for Avon, Barnet, Bedfordshire, Berkshire, Cambridgeshire, Hertfordshire, Hillingdon, Lambeth, Lewisham, Wakefield and Westminster LEAs; the Church of England Diocesan Advisers; the Shap Working Party on World Religions in Education; the Association of Religious Educational Advisers and Inspectors; Bristol University; and a number of individual schools. These have generated great interest in this approach and helped to refine its conceptual basis.

Many of the recipes in this book were demonstrated in a series of courses on food and faith, entitled 'You are what you eat!': Father John Lee (Russian Orthodox Christian), 'Ba' Katbamna and Nelini Nanso (Hindu), and Parsan Kaur and Harbans Singh (Sikh) have kindly agreed for their family and community recipes to be reproduced here. 'Homing In' also owes a tremendous debt to Kanta Gomez, Samira Habashi, Kanwaljit Kaur-Singh, Usha Malhotra and Indira Sen who combined their professional expertise as educators with depth of insight and clarity of expression when conveying the essence of home life in their traditions.

The project has been rooted throughout in concrete classroom realities and those teachers who generously shared the fruits of their experience, offered additional expertise and stimulated many improvements, are sadly too numerous to mention.

But very special thanks go to the children, parents and staff of those Hounslow schools who bravely and imaginatively trialled the project over an extensive experimental period – especially Chatsworth Infants, Cranford Infants, Berkeley Juniors, Sparrow Farm Infants and Wellington Primary.

CONTENTS

'Homing In' is a new approach to religious education in the primary years: it has been developed in response to the needs of teachers who want to enrich children's experiences in creative play spaces – 'pretend areas', or 'home corners' – and offer them opportunities to explore some of the ways that families express their religious faith within the home.

This approach enables children to enter imaginatively into a coherent way of life; to encounter beliefs and values in their most natural context; to appreciate the significance of the most cherished objects of a faith tradition; and to engage in a range of learning about themselves, other people and the material world.

The objects which have been generated derive from genuine religious artefacts, yet are of a size and substance which children can handle easily and safely. They provide the teacher with a flexible resource for extending topic work and for creating a specific kind of home within the 'pretend area'.

The 'Homing In' approach is characterised by the following features and purposes:

Experiential
It builds on children's natural impulse to explore reality and to represent the world they discover in a variety of dramatic forms, including make-believe and ritualised behaviour. Play is how young children work... and, by assuming roles in the context of a specific religious 'home', they can develop empathy while remaining fully themselves.

Affirming
Bringing homes actually into the classroom demonstrates the value that the school places on children's personal lives, upholds their culture and eases their transition to school. It provides children with a chance to reflect privately on their domestic environment and can lead to greater self-awareness and a heightened self-image. Children who are involved in setting up a 'home' – and act as hosts to other children whose circumstances differ – are able to share their inside knowledge and skills, and are seen in a giving role; this further enhances their esteem and self-respect.

Extending
'Starting where the child is' – but not ending there – underlies this approach: children's views are enlarged through their vicarious engagement in lifestyles which may resonate with their own yet are likely to differ in significant ways.

Social
This approach is essentially interactional: adopting appropriate roles, assuming certain codes of behaviour and enacting specific rituals opens up new possibilities for children to interact with others.

Cross-curricular

It can be used to expand and enliven many classroom topics and integrate all National Curriculum subjects and many realms of learning. The whole is greater than some of its parts... and much is gained when seemingly discrete aspects of the curriculum are brought together in fresh combinations. Teachers involved in the 'Homing In' project experienced this as a process of growth for themselves as well for their pupils.

Linguistic

'Homing In' stimulates and supports a wide range of language learning. It involves much speaking and listening in the negotiation of home situations and the communication of deep levels of meaning. Handling replicas of holy scriptures – and appreciating the way in which they are valued within the faith tradition – often serves to accentuate children's respect for, and desire to achieve, literacy. Bilingual pupils frequently come into their own and all pupils come to appreciate the world of languages.

Technological

The 'Homing In' experience is essentially tactile for in most religious homes certain objects are endowed with special meaning and are actively employed to recall important events, to crystallise the individual's identity, to bond the community and to express what is most deeply valued within the tradition. Children are thereby presented with phenomena which are cherished for their physical form yet transcend the merely materialistic.

Traditional artefacts are created with tremendous care: typically, they conform to an established form or pattern which requires discipline, yet paradoxically permits individual creativity within the overall 'design brief'. This makes them ideal models for technological investigations within the classroom. Many of the artefacts in this collection can be made by children, with some supervision, and offer great scope for problem-solving activities involving mathematical, scientific and technological concepts and skills. The children derive great satisfaction – and a sense of ownership – when they can set up their 'home' with things they have made themselves.

Authentic

This approach helps children to 'get into' a cultural or religious system and begin to see it 'from the inside'. It can complement thematic approaches which present features of separate religions and cultures as a part of an overall human scheme. Indeed, the over-arching themes here are homes, families, 'ourselves', 'the special'...

Diverse

The realisation of what makes homes both similar and different endorses that which is essentially human as well as that which testifies to the infinite variety and richness of humankind: this perspective emphasises both respect for 'the other' and respect for 'my own' – which is equally relevant in 'multicultural' and 'monocultural' schools.

Religious

'Homing In' is clearly a vehicle for religious education yet knowledge of explicit religious phenomena is only one of its positive outcomes. It also creates an arena in which implicit religious values – such as worship and celebration, awe and mystery, right and wrong – can be identified and explored, and through which children's own views of life may be mirrored.

Chapter 2 **MOVING IN**

The first step to take is the decision about which home to 'move into' – and why... The project has been trialled in a range of classrooms and the choice of 'first homes' has depended on several factors. A particular 'home' might be chosen because most of the pupils are members of that faith and the teacher is able to signal the place their religious culture has in the class; or because only some of the pupils are faith members, acting 'at home' to the others – whose turn will come later. When they are in a school with no faith members at all of the home chosen, the 'home corner' acts as a living museum for that faith.

Whatever the reason and whatever the situation, it is important to ensure that 'Homing In' has a clear and coherent place within the curriculum, and the possibilities for this are almost infinite. On pages 14-15, 46-47, 70-71, 102-103, 132-133 there are ten 'doorways' – two for each of the five faiths represented in this book – in the form for webs for topics which are quite frequently explored in primary schools. They indicate the range of learning which the approach can generate and also how it can become the focus for an exploration of home life within a specific faith. For each faith, one of the 'doorways' is 'generic' in the sense that it might equally be used with any faith. The other 'doorway' is 'specific' in the sense that it best relates to that particular faith and actually leads pupils to the heart of that tradition more than to any other.

The particular cultural manifestations of these five world-wide faiths are drawn from those most commonly experienced in Britain: this is an important starting-point for pupils and lays firm foundations for their later understanding of the faith's diversity.

Intellectual preparation for the teacher is as important here as with any new programme: the chapters entitled 'Being in a Christian Home', 'Being in a Hindu Home', 'Being in a Jewish Home', 'Being in a Muslim Home' and 'Being in a Sikh Home' are intended to give some flavour of family life within those traditions, and the bibliography and list of useful addresses (on pages 149 and 151) suggest resources through which teachers and pupils can supplement that knowledge. Human resources are always more alive and more immediate than written material, and every opportunity to learn from an adherent of the faith – whether a pupil, parent, member of staff or a formal representative of the community – should be welcomed with open arms. The 'Homing In' project discovered that faith community members were delighted to be involved, and they willingly shared their experiences, insights and expertise in response to every invitation.

Feeling at home

Very occasionally parents express their concern about this approach: they may be worried that their children are being led into the unknown

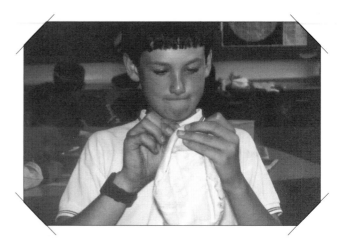

and will become somehow unrecognisable. The contrary is the case: the pupils themselves were never confused about their identity and, perhaps precisely because they had an opportunity to be closely involved, never muddled one faith with another – which sometimes happens in more formal approaches to religious education. Parents need to understand that 'Homing In' is not at all an attempt at 'multiple conversion' but an engaging way for pupils to learn about people in their world, as well as about themselves. Parents – as well as pupils and teachers – deserve to see that this is an integral part of the curriculum and any fears they might have can be allayed if they are invited to observe, participate in or contribute to the programme. A concrete way of involving parents is through the manufacture of the artefacts, many of which can be made by children with some supervision but some of which require skill, knowledge and dexterity that only an adult has developed. Parents who are asked to use their particular interests and talents – or work with children in the classroom – immediately see not only that the approach is non-threatening but also that it has tremendous all-round benefits.

Teachers who, because of their own sensitivities or their sensitivities to the feelings of parents, may initially be reluctant to set up a religious home corner can begin by viewing 'Homing In' as an artefact project to complement more conventional approaches to RE: the benefits of that approach are still considerable. The artefacts can illustrate stories and demonstrations of rituals and, as confidence grows, be employed in role play which may eventually lead to a fully-fledged home corner. This is a useful line of development for any teacher to consider, even if there is great enthusiasm and confidence at the outset.

It is very important – as with any role play situation – to help children to 'de-role' – that is, to 'return' or come out of role – at the end of a period in the home corner. There are many

strategies for this but, these are simple, effective and satisfying:

with all the children sitting in a circle:

- ask each child, in turn, to say, 'I am (own name)' and ask other children to say, 'He/she is (that child's name).'
- ask each child to say, 'I was (name of role) and I am (own name).'

Some teachers have successfully created and used artefacts to set up a museum of a particular faith in their classroom. While providing a certain emotional distance which may be desirable, this fulfils many of the aims of the 'Homing In' approach and has other educational gains. It has involved the children in labelling, mounting and ordering artefacts; in creating museum catalogues (with simple text and illustrations); and acting as museum guides (for example, to parents and to other children in their own or another class). 'Guiding' motivates children to gain knowledge and insight into the particular artefacts and their use, and also gives them experience of the role of 'expert'. Some museums have also featured a shop, with souvenirs to buy, such as stickers (that is, decorated self-adhesive labels), bookmarks and the like, crafted by the children. These situations give children valuable opportunities to rehearse or reinforce appropriate museum and shop behaviour, including handling money. Artefact shops in other classrooms have produced similar benefits and the shopkeepers have given the shoppers advice on suitable artefacts to buy as gifts for wedding couples or for new-born babies.

Using the resources in this book

Each of the five chapters on religious homes has five sections:

1. Being in a ... Home

These sections give some basic knowledge and insight into the characteristics of family life and the religious practices of the home. Both adults and children who are unfamiliar with a particular faith tradition may refer to further information or consult faith community members.

Each of these sections has a grid of eight pictures (that is, on pages 10-11, 42-43, 66-67, 98-99 and 128-129). These grids can serve a curricular purpose as well: they can be photocopied ad infinitum and cut up to make picture cards for a range of remembering, naming and coordination activities, for example, 'snap', pairs or picture dominoes.

Each of these sections also has a large picture depicting a family scene (that is, on pages 12-13, 44-45, 68-69, 100-101, 130-131): each can be copied and used as a poster or cut up to make a jigsaw. As with all the designs in this book, it is best to refer to the colour photographs on the cover or to consult reference works or 'human resources' for authentic colours.

2. Doorways to a ... Home
These sections suggest some curricular links and starting points for the teacher.

3. 'Furnishings'
These sections are the largest, and give illustrations and full instructions for the manufacture of the artefacts – including clothes for children or, in the case of the Christian home, for dolls. Some also have templates which need to be traced or copied and then cut out. A 'clean' photocopier is important for those designs which are going to be coloured and form part of the artefact itself. The best adhesive, unless otherwise stated, is PVA, available from stationers and craft suppliers: for some of the artefacts, it is also used as a translucent varnish or water-proofer. Many artefacts can be made with recyclable materials.

4. Food
Each of these sections contains three recipes: one for bread, and two others – mostly one savoury dish and one sweet dish. Although not all the faith traditions in this book are vegetarian, many do have a vegetarian repertoire and recipes have been chosen from these so that as many children and adults as possible may taste them! Some recipes need only cold cooking and many can be made by the children with adult supervision or by adults with child participation. The recipes make enough for a class of up to 30 children and some adults to taste.

5. Books
These sections contain some simplified, paraphrased extracts from each tradition's scriptural or liturgical texts. Each paragraph or verse, in large print, can form one page. It is important to bind the books in the appropriate format for the specific faith tradition, that is, as landscape or portrait, opening left-to-right or right-to-left. The correct format in each case is given below and in the relevant 'Being in a ... home' section. Any and every bookmaking technique is suitable for this but the simplest is as follows:

1. Type or write neatly each paragraph or verse on to an A5 sheet (half A4 paper or thin card – either white or cream coloured; use landscape format for the Sikh book and portrait format for all the others. If making multiple copies, create an original of two verses/paragraphs on one A4 sheet, photocopy and cut in half.

2. Paste or spray glue two sheets together, back to back, to form a leaf of the book. Repeat with all the pages.

3. Cut a sheet of A4 thick card in half, to create a front and back cover (each A5 in size). The covers may be edged with ribbon or flat cord.

4. Using a hole puncher, make two holes in each page and both covers – on the appropriate edges.

5. Line up the pages and covers appropriately: the Christian, Hindu and Sikh books should open from left to right and the Jewish and Muslim books from right to left.

6. Thread a ribbon or length of cord through the holes and tie in a bow.

7. Label the books with the appropriate title, either in handwriting (using black or gold pens) or with appliqué letters (e.g. Letraset).

Chapter 3 **BEING IN A CHRISTIAN HOME**

When the 'Home Team' was discussing the religious characteristics of home life with members of various faith communities (see 'Moving In' on page 3), Christians invariably had great difficulty in articulating their own home's Christian characteristics – and this itself proved to be an interesting point of discussion. It emerged that it is often difficult to identify the 'Christian-ness' of many Christian homes in Britain today for at least four reasons:

- Being Christian is often associated with British-ness because of Christianity's historic role in, and enduring influence on, British culture. For example, many Christians mentioned their Christmas celebrations at home as examples of their religious life but, almost in the same breath as it were, acknowledged that many people in Britain who are not Christian also celebrate Christmas at home.

- For many Christians, religion is more church oriented than home-oriented; it is practised more within the local religious community than in the context of family life: as a result, their home may be indistinguishable, except perhaps on occasions of heightened spiritual significance, from the home of a secular family. Nevertheless, there are certain well-established regular and recurring routines and rituals which are characteristic of traditional Christianity in many homes, including 'Grace' before and after meals, Bible reading and set or extemporaneous prayer, say, in the morning or evening. Many Christian families are renewing or evolving new practices in the home.

- The practise of Christianity is very diverse not only because of its wide geographical spread and its cultural diversity but also because of its denominational variations. Thus, in terms of practice, many Christians interviewed were hesitant to label their practices as 'Christian' in the universal sense.

- In some Christian groups, as a matter of principle, there is a greater emphasis on belief than on ritual behaviour and there are, in particular, few or no artefacts commonly or regularly used. This means that there are relatively few signs of uniquely Christian practice and no immediate signs of Christian-ness at home.

Notwithstanding these hesitations, *Homing In* identifies certain common if not central practices, and their corresponding artefacts. The rosary, holy water stoop, Brigid's cross, and First Communion doll's dress and 'photograph', for example, are drawn from the Roman Catholic tradition, especially as it is experienced by families of Irish origin in Britain. The Chi Rho mobile and the 'God is a Spirit' card derive from expressions of Evangelical Protestant Christianity and reflect its emphasis on word and text. The prayer book is specially Anglican.

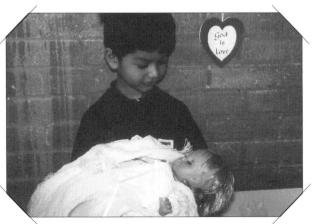

Ikons, originating and enduring in the Orthodox tradition, are today used by many Roman Catholics and Anglicans. Christians are united in their acceptance of the Bible but it is generally more actively used by Anglicans and Free Church members than other Christian groups. Other artefacts, for example, the Baptismal candle and the doll's christening dress are used in more than one denomination.

Purists would argue that denominational differences should not be fudged in setting up a Christian home so that, since teachers would not provide or permit a copy of the Qur'an (Islamic) and a murti (Hindu) together in the same 'home', they should not provide or permit Roman Catholic and Evangelical artefacts together in the same home. However, practitioners would suggest that it is adequate, and may be developmentally appropriate, for children to recognise Christian-ness.

Through missionary activity and the dissemination of western culture over many centuries, Christianity is today the most widely practised religion and is present in every country in the world. Across the world, it has assumed a wide range of cultural forms. In many resources on Christianity, Christians are portrayed as white but in reality the majority of the world's Christians are black or brown. It is important that images of Christians reflect Christianity's ethnic diversity.

It is important to appreciate the diversity of beliefs and practices shared by Christians across the world. Many of these distinctions are denominational in character and have important historical roots. There is also, as within any tradition, a range of individual perspectives and emphases: these factors make it particularly difficult to say 'most Christians'. Although there are thousands of denominations, it may be helpful for pupils to understand that:

• there are four main groups or families of Christians: Orthodox, Roman Catholic, Protestant and Pentecostal, and the biggest group (in terms of numbers of adherents) is Roman Catholic;

• some 'movements' within Christianity span several denominations, for example the charismatic movement;

• there are new denominations (sometimes called cults or sects) which depart from conventional practices but have much in common with mainstream churches;

• especially in matters of belief, the similarities between the families or groupings of Christians are greater than the differences;

• although 'organised' Christianity is less significant to people in western society today, western culture and, to some extent the cultures of countries which have been colonised by western countries or otherwise affected by western imperialism, continue to be shaped by its Christian history;

• Christian affiliation remains firm in other parts of the world and, in some cases, is growing or being revived, for example in former Communist countries.

It is also important to appreciate that, for many people in the west, the term 'Christian' may be used loosely. Many people may call themselves Christian while not subscribing to Christian beliefs or observing Christian practices: the term 'people of vague faith' has been coined by the religious media to refer to them. Some people use the word 'Christian' to mean 'well behaved' or 'traditional' – or even 'British' or 'white'. In *Homing In*, the word 'Christian' is only used of people who hold Christian beliefs and observe Christian practices – however varied they may be.

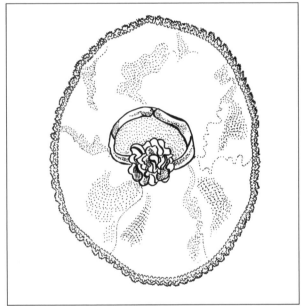

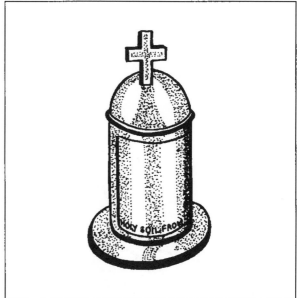

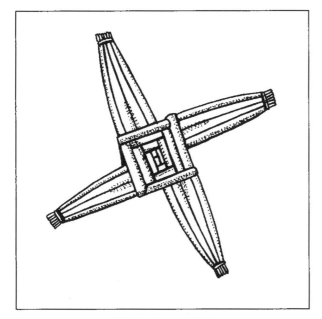

God
is
Love

God is the spirit
and people who
worship God must
worship him in
spirit and in
truth.

2. DOORWAYS TO A CHRISTIAN HOME

SHAPES AND CROSSES
specific to Christianity

English
- shape vocabulary
- reading and writing stories and poems about shapes
- shape in letter- and word-formation in handwriting

Mathematics
- sorting, naming and matching shapes
- matching crosses
- measuring crosses
- right angles

Science
- sorting natural objects by shape
- patterns in nature
- weathering on crosses outside
- materials used to make crosses

Technology
- making crosses and crucifixes
- use of shape in design, including strong and weak shapes

History
- ancient and modern crosses

Geography
- location of churches in area
- the use of crosses and crucifixes in church and other architecture

Art
- printing symbols
- shape pictures
- weaving
- patchwork and tessellation
- appreciating the image of the cross in paintings and other art forms

Music
- appreciating shape in music
- listening to Christian music on the theme of crosses and crucifixes

Physical education
- playing 'statues'
- creating tableaux or 'sculpts' for given or chosen shapes
- shape games involving moving in different shapes

Religious education
- varied styles of crosses and crucifixes e.g. Celtic, Latin, Orthodox, Maltese, Jerusalem...
- reading Christian stories about crosses and crucifixes
- significance of cross as Christian symbol
- national and other flags which feature crosses
- making Brigid's cross and other crosses shape 'hunt' in churches

BABIES
generic but with emphasis on Christianity

English
- ❑ stories about birth and babies
- ❑ discussion about impressions of babies
- ❑ home corner role play involving a 'baby'
- ❑ writing invitations to christening and thank you letters for presents received

Mathematics
- ❑ graphs and charts of average number of children in family
- ❑ boy/girl probability
- ❑ growth rates
- ❑ data handling of birth weights and lengths

Science
- ❑ investigation of sounds in rattles
- ❑ handling a real baby
- ❑ babies' health needs
- ❑ breast-feeding and bottle-feeding life cycle

Technology
- ❑ designing and making babies' toys and books
- ❑ designing and making artefacts as gifts for a Christian baby
- ❑ making christening cake

History
- ❑ babies in the past and present, gleaned from photographs and oral history
- ❑ child care and approaches to child-rearing in different eras

Geography
- ❑ child care and approaches to child-rearing in different cultures and settings

Art
- ❑ creating pictures and mobiles for babies
- ❑ christening scene display
- ❑ portraits of babies and their families
- ❑ creating realis for christening souvenir book

Music
- ❑ learning songs about babies
- ❑ songs for babies and young children, including finger rhymes and lullabies

Physical education
- ❑ imitating baby movements

Religious education
- ❑ stories about the birth and childhood of exemplars in various traditions
- ❑ naming rituals in Christian and other traditions
- ❑ simulation of infant baptism (christening)
- ❑ artefacts in baptism, including font, holy water and christening robes
- ❑ vows of parents and godparents, and role of priest or minister

3.'FURNISHINGS'

BAPTISMAL CANDLE

What you need

- inner tube of kitchen roll (the thinner the better)
- photocopy of motif (two examples given)
- red, blue and gold pens
- scraps of yellow or orange tissue
- white paper, if necessary

What you do

1. If tube is not white, cover with white paper.

2. Colour motif as follows: anchor – red with a gold cross; waves – blue, divided by gold lines; drops of water – blue; rays from the dove – gold.

3. Stick motif to tube.

4. Attach flame-shaped pieces of tissue to top.

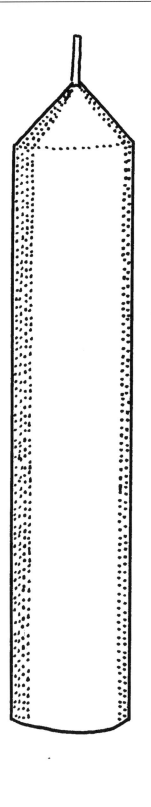

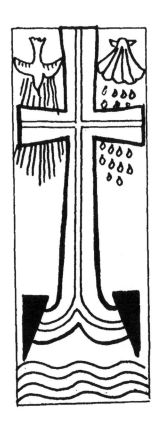

CERTIFICATES OF BAPTISM AND CONFIRMATION

Before the certificates are framed, details relating to a real or hypothetical person should be filled in. The symbols may be tinted: the flame should be red or yellow; the Chi Rho gold; the dove and the shell white.

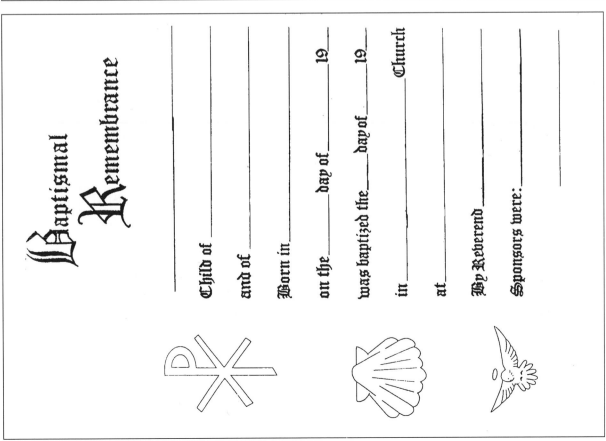

FIRST COMMUNION PHOTOGRAPH

Many Roman Catholic homes feature a photograph – usually in a prominent place – taken of a child on the day he or she made their First Communion. If it is not possible to borrow one of these, the drawings in this book – one of a white girl and one of a black boy – may be used. The background is likely to be fairly neutral and the frame may be of any colour – though the use of gold/silver pens would be effective. The boy would probably wear a white shirt, dark trousers, tie and shoes, and a red rosette. The girl would be dressed entirely in white with a gold or silver crucifix; the flowers she is carrying may be coloured.

DOLL'S DRESSES FOR CHRISTENING AND FIRST COMMUNION

These garments fit a 40 cm baby doll. They can only be made by someone with basic dressmaking skills.

PETTICOAT FOR CHRISTENING GOWN

What you need

- template of pieces A and B
- 75cm white polyester/cotton, 120cm wide
- white bias tape
- 150cm narrow white lace trim
- white sewing thread

What you do

1. Photocopy templates.
2. Fold material in half lengthways.
3. For skirt, cut off piece measuring 50cm.
4. Place piece A on fold, and cut.
5. Cut piece B.
6. Neaten all edges and allow a seam of 0.5cm throughout.
7. Join pieces A (front bodice) and B (back bodice) together across shoulders and under armholes.
8. Stitch the length of the skirt, leaving an opening of 6cm at the top.
9. Gather round the waist and join to bodice.
10. Turn back opening 0.5cm, turn again and stitch.
11. Edge neck and armholes with bias tape.
12. Turn bottom hem and edge with lace.
13. Sew press stud fasteners to back opening.

Christening petticoat (back view)

CHRISTENING GOWN

What you need

- 75cm white organdie or net curtaining, 120cm wide

- 1m narrow white lace trim

- narrow elastic

- white sewing thread

- two press stud fasteners

What you do

1. Follow cutting instructions for petticoat, adding piece C (sleeve: cut twice).

2. As for petticoat, join front and back bodice together, make skirt, gather waist and join to bodice.

3. Turn bottom edge of sleeves 0.5 cm, turn again and sew.

4. Slip stitch lace to under edge of sleeves.

5. Thread elastic through and pull to required size.

6. Machine sleeve seams with right sides together.

7. Gather top of sleeves and ease into armholes.

8. Turn back opening as for petticoat.

9. Finish neck with bias strip of material and edge with lace.

10. Turn hem and sew press stud fasteners to back opening.

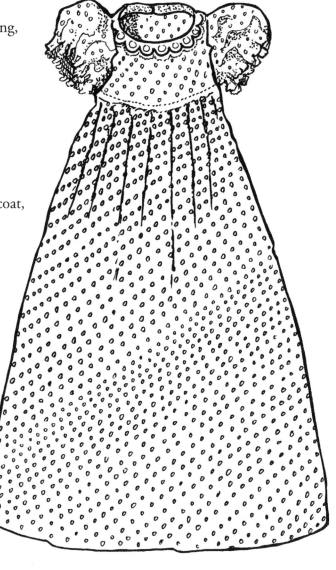

FIRST COMMUNION DRESS

What you need

- 1m broderie anglaise with scalloped edges, 40cm wide
- 75cm narrow white satin ribbon (for sash)
- white sewing thread
- white bias tape
- narrow elastic
- two press stud fasteners

What you do

1. Use the same pattern as the christening gown but add 2cm in length to pieces A and B (front and back bodice) and 9cm to piece C (sleeve).

2. For the skirt, cut a lengthways strip 20cm wide.

3. From the remaining strip, cut two sleeves by placing bottom edge of piece C on scalloped edge of fabric.

4. Cut bodice pieces.

5. Sew shoulders seams.

6. On wrong side, place a bias strip 1cm from bottom edge of sleeve: machine both edges of bias strip.

7. Through this, thread elastic, adjust to size and fasten off.

8. Gather top of sleeves and ease into armholes.

9. Join back and front bodice together by one seam running from bottom sleeve to waist.

10. Finish neck with a bias strip.

11. Join the skirt at the back, leaving an opening of 6cm.

12. Gather at the top and join to bodice.

13. Turn back opening 0.5cm, turn again and stitch.

14. Finish with two press stud fasteners and tie white satin sash.

SLIP FOR FIRST COMMUNION DRESS

What you need

- 1m white polyester/cotton, 20cm wide
- 1m white narrow lace trim
- length of elastic
- white sewing thread

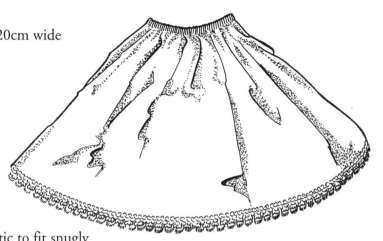

What you do

1. Join sides together.
2. Turn top 0.5cm, turn again and stitch.
3. Thread through enough elastic to fit snugly around doll's waist, and secure.
4. Turn hem at top and edge with lace.

FIRST COMMUNION VEIL

What you need

- 20cm white satin ribbon, 2.5 cm wide
- circle of white tulle or stiff netting, 30cm in diameter
- white sewing thread
- small white silk flower, approximately 5cm in diameter

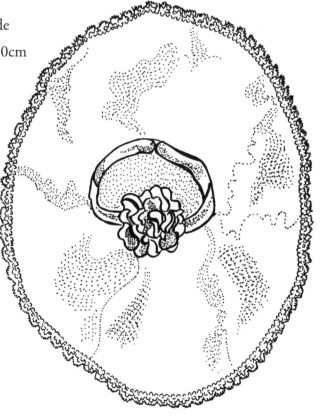

What you do

1. To make band, fold over ribbon and stitch.
2. Thread elastic through ribbon, adjust to doll's head and secure.
3. Edge tulle circle with lace.
4. Fold over about one third: slip stitch this fold to middle of band.
5. Finish with flower in the centre.

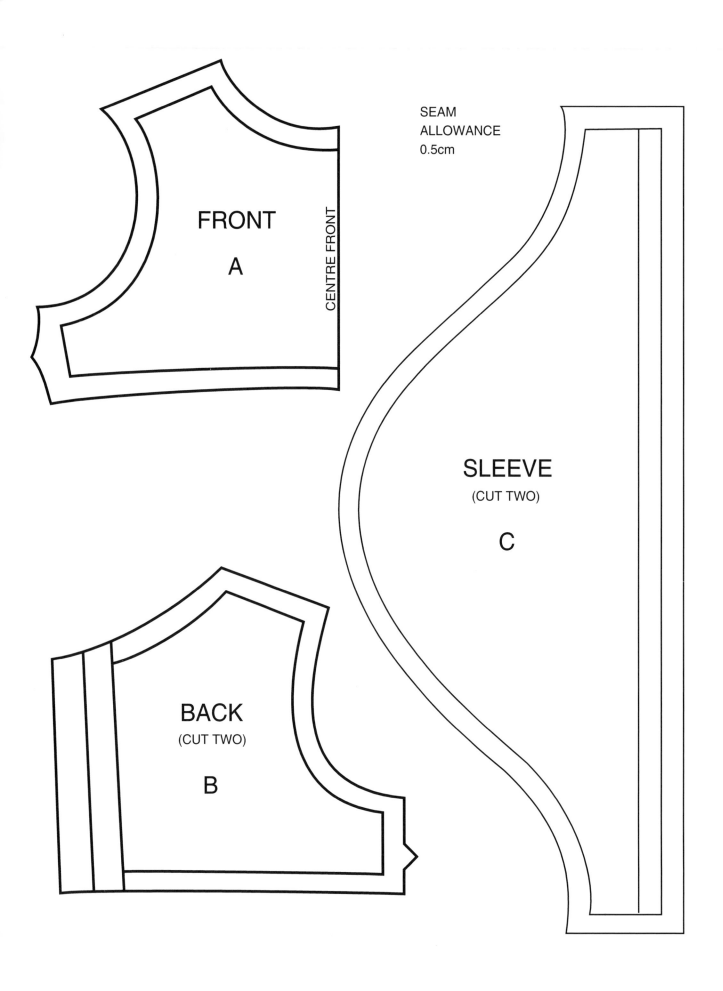

SEAM
ALLOWANCE
0.5cm

FRONT

A

CENTRE FRONT

SLEEVE

(CUT TWO)

C

BACK

(CUT TWO)

B

IKON

(sacred image)

What you need

- an ikon reproduction picture, such as a postcard from an art shop, church shop or a Christmas card; if unavailable, use photocopy of an ikon from this book

- piece of wood, about 5mm thick, cut to exactly the same size as the ikon picture used

- very strong, cold tea

- clean paint brush

- PVA

What you do

1. Stain the sides of the wood by applying several coats of tea. Leave to dry.

2. Mount the ikon picture on to the wood and leave to dry.

3. To give the ikon picture a sheen, apply several coats of PVA glue.

Note

If using photocopy, cut out and colour in muted tones, except for the halos and letters which should be gold or silver. Then cover it with clear contact film – to achieve the varnished effect – before mounting it on the tea-stained wood.

TRIPTYCH

What you need

- template of three 'ikon' pictures
- thin card
- gold card or shiny paper
- masking tape
- clear contact film
- PVA

What you do

1. Photocopy the pictures (they may be reduced to half size).
2. Colour the pictures in muted tones (dull gold, silver or brass, or brown or grey) to obtain 'antique' effect.
3. Glue pictures to thin cards and cut out carefully.
4. Cover pictures with clear contact film.
5. Using the mounted pictures as templates, cut a cover for the triptych in the gold card.
6. Join pictures together at rear with masking tape.
7. Back triptych with gold card.

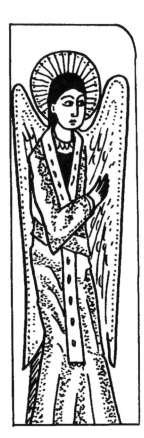

HOLY WATER STOOP

What you need

- Blessed Virgin Mary or Sacred Heart motif
- thin white A4 card
- clear contact film
- short piece of string or cord
- If a 3-D stoop which can hold water is required, a small plastic yogurt (or similar) pot can be attached. It should be preferably be of a plain colour and triangular or semicircular in shape with one flat side: the most suitable is the smaller of the pair from a yogurt and fruit combination dessert, sold in most supermarkets. You will also need some strong glue for sticking the plastic pot to the stoop.
- PVA

What you do

1. Photocopy motif and colour carefully: the Blessed Virgin Mary is traditionally dressed in blue or gold and the Sacred Heart in red, white and gold.

2. Mount motif onto thin card and cut it out carefully.

3. Cover with clear contact film.

4. Attach a loop of string to back of stoop for hanging.

5. If making 3D, cut away water container shape at bottom 0f template. Glue pot to bottom of figure and apply firm pressure.

ROSARY

(prayer beads)

What you need

- six large identical beads (approximately 0.75cm in diameter)
- 53 small identical beads (0.5cm or less in diameter)
- small crucifix (approximately 1.5cm long) – available from many churches, Christian book shops and repositories
- strong thread

What you do

1. Thread the beads following the detail on the picture: there should be five groups of ten small beads, punctuated by a large bead.
2. Join the two ends of the thread by passing them through a large bead.
3. Holding both threads together, thread on three small beads and one large bead.
4. Attach the crucifix with a firm but neat knot.

HOLY LAND SOIL RECEPTACLE

What you need

- clear plastic drum from 35mm film
- two matches
- strong clear glue
- about one teaspoonful of soil
- craft knife or fine saw

What you do

1. Cut off sulphur tips using sharp craft knife or fine saw.
2. In the centre of the lid of the film drum, make a hole large enough for a match to be pushed in tightly.
3. Lay one match across the other above the middle point to form crucifix. Apply glue and allow to dry.
4. Fill drum with soil and replace lid.
5. Attach crucifix to lid of film drum and stick with glue. Allow to dry.

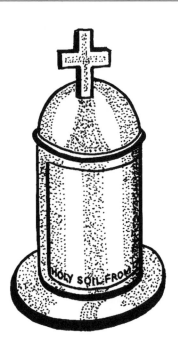

BRIGID'S CROSS

What you need

- 16 pipe cleaners, cream or corn coloured

- matching thread

What you do

1. Fold all pipe cleaners in half and divide into four groups of four.

2. Using one group of four, loop one pipe cleaner into the other at a right angle; loop the third into the second at a right angle, pointing in the opposite direction to the first; loop the fourth pipe cleaner into the third at a right angle pointing in the opposite direction from the second. This forms an asymmetrical cross shape. Ease four loops together and hold firmly.

3. Repeat with the other three groups of pipe cleaners.

4. Tie four corners of cross with thread and trim ends.

5. Use thread to make loop for hanging.

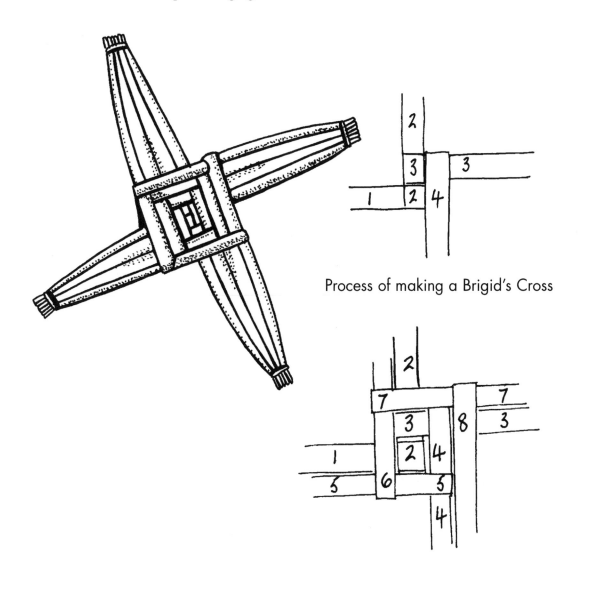

Process of making a Brigid's Cross

CATACOMB CROSS

What you need

- template of catacomb cross
- small length of chain (such as used for basin plugs) or grey thread or cord
- pale grey colouring pencil (or lead pencil)
- bottle green colouring pencil
- small piece of thick card
- PVA

What you do

1. Photocopy template and stick onto card.
2. Colour background of cross grey.
3. Colour small patches of the letters and images green to achieve a mottled, 'antique' effect; fill in remaining patches grey.
4. Cut out cross.
5. Attach chain or cord to hang.

WALL CRUCIFIX

What you need

- templates of crucifixes A and B
- thin brown card
- clear contact film
- short piece of thin card
- PVA

What you do

1. Photocopy template of crucifix A, and cut out.
2. Photocopy crucifix B on to thin brown card or draw round template onto thin brown card; cut out.
3. Mount A and B (this will give a brown border of about 3mm).
4. Cover with clear contact film.
5. Attach loop of cord at back for hanging.

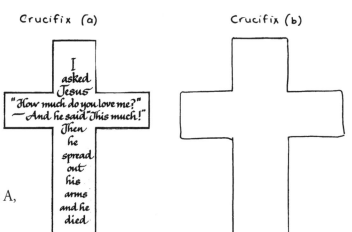

Crucifix (a)   Crucifix (b)

A

'GOD IS LOVE' TEXT CARD

What you need

- templates A and B
- piece of thin red card
- short piece of thin cord
- clear contact film
- PVA

What you do

1. Photocopy design A on to red card and cut out.

2. Photocopy design B on to white paper and cut out.

3. Paste design B onto design A: this will give it a red border all the way round.

4. Cover with clear contact film.

5. Attach a loop of cord to the back, for hanging.

B

God
is
Love

CHI RHO MOBILE

What you need

- templates of designs A, B and C

- 2 sheets of A4 pale blue card

- 1 sheet of A4 white card

- pale blue embroidery thread

- PVA

What you do

1. Make two photocopies of design A (Chi Rho) on blue card and cut out.

2. Cut a piece of embroidery thread: the mobile will hang from the ceiling so the length of the thread will depend on the height of the room.

3. Glue the two blue pieces of card back to back (with the same side up!) with the length of thread between them: allow 15cm of thread to extend below.

4. Make one photocopy of designs B and C (dove), and cut out.

5. Glue B and C back to back, with the bottom of the 15cm length between them.

A

Christ for the World

The World for Christ

B

B

'SPIRIT' TEXT CARD

What you need

- templates of 'flames' A, B and C
- red paper
- thin yellow card
- clear contact film
- PVA
- short piece of cord for hanging or small piece of thick cardboard for 'stand'

A

God is the spirit and people who worship God must worship him in spirit and in truth.

C

What you do

1. Photocopy 'flame' A on to white paper, 'flame' B on to red paper and C on to thin yellow card; cut each out.

2. Paste A on to B and A/B on to C: this double-mounting will give a narrow border round each.

3. If hanging, cover with clear contact film; then attach a loop of cord to the back of the 'flame'.

4. If 'standing', fold under the 'flame' about 0.5cm and on the underside glue a strip of thick card. Cover the whole 'flame' and the stand with clear contact film.

4. FOOD

BREAD

Bread is a staple food in many cultures. In the Christian tradition, bread also has a spiritual and symbolic significance. Jesus said 'I am the Bread of Life', and bread is at the heart of the central Christian celebration of Eucharist or Mass. Christians, like followers of other religions, celebrate harvest festival. When they gather together in church to thank God for this bounty, all kinds of produce, brought as gifts, are displayed. The centrepiece of the display is often a large loaf baked in the shape of a wheat sheaf or other harvest symbol. This recipe can be adapted if the loaf is required for this purpose.

What you need

- 3 cups plain flour (bleached, wholemeal or a mixture of both)
- 1 tablespoon fresh yeast or 2 teaspoons of dried yeast
- 1 cup warm water
- 1 teaspoon sugar
- 1 teaspoon salt
- a little butter or oil
- a little milk for glazing (optional)

What you do

1. Mix the yeast with 1/2 a cup of warm water and the sugar.

2. Put 2 cups of flour and the salt into a bowl and make a 'well' in the centre with your fist.

3. Pour in the yeast and sprinkle with flour, and leave in a warm place until the yeast froths.

4. Pour in 1/2 cup of warm water and mix well with floury hands into a smooth lump.

5. Cover the bowl with a clean cloth and leave in a warm place for about 45 minutes: the dough will double in size during this time.

6. Place the dough on a floured board and knead thoroughly!

7. Place the dough in a loaf tin (rubbed with butter or oil) or shape the dough as required – either as a cottage loaf, rolls, plaited loaf or to resemble a wheat sheaf, and place on an oiled baking tray.

8. Heat the oven to Gas Mark 8 or 450°F.

9. Allow the dough to rise for a further 45 minutes.

10. Glaze the loaf with milk before baking for a more attractive result!

11. Place in the hot oven and leave to bake for 10 minutes.

12. After ten minutes, reduce the heat to Gas Mark 4 or 350°F.

13. Check the bread after 45 minutes and remove when it is ready.

14. Allow bread to cool.

CIRNI PASCHA
(Easter Cheese)

This is a Russian Orthodox dish. It is a great family favourite, prepared and eaten especially on the evening of Easter Day but also throughout the forty days following Easter, until Ascension Thursday. It is not made or eaten at any other time of the year. Russian Christians always decorate the cheese with crosses and the letters XB ('Christ is Risen'/'Kristos Voskreses').

What you need
- 450g cream cheese
- 225g unsalted butter
- 1 cup cottage cheese
- 1 cup sugar
- 3/4 cup candied mixed fruit
- 1/3 cup slivered almonds
- 1/3 cup raisins
- yolks of 12 hard boiled eggs
- large, clean clay flower pot
- muslin

What you do
1. Blend together the cheeses, butter and sugar for about 20 minutes.
2. Reserve some of the candied fruit for decoration.
3. Add the rest of the fruit, with the nuts and raisins, to the cheese mixture. Blend well.
4. Add the egg yolks and thoroughly mix all together.
5. Line a mould (such as a clean, large clay flower pot) with muslin.
6. Spoon in the mixture and pack it down.
7. Wrap the muslin over the top.
8. Weight it down.
9. Set it in a pan to drain in the fridge for about 48 hours.
10. Drain off the water in the pan from time to time.
11. Unmould the cheese onto a plate and decorate with candied fruits.

CELEBRATION CAKE
This recipe for a rich fruit cake can be used to make celebration cakes for a variety of occasions.

CHRISTMAS CAKE
This would normally be prepared and decorated before Christmas and then served on the day itself, often as the centrepiece of the tea table. Slices of the cake will often be served in the days that follow.

WEDDING CAKE
This is prepared and decorated in advance of the wedding itself. It often consists of several tiers, supported by little pillars (available in cake shops). The wedding cake is an important feature of the reception for guests which follows most Christian (as well as secular) weddings in western society. At the end of the celebration meal, the bride and groom are invited to ceremonially cut the cake. Speeches and toasts to the couple then follow, and the cake is sliced and distributed to guests. Any well-wishers unable to attend the wedding might be posted a slice of cake in a small box, specifically designed for this purpose and available from stationers.

CHRISTENING CAKE
It is traditional for western Christian couples to preserve the top tier of their wedding cake to be re-iced later on, to form the christening cake of their first child. Christenings are usually followed by a gathering for family, friends and other guests held at home, with refreshments provided. The cake will be at the centre of this celebration. A toast will be made to the baby wishing him/her, health, happiness and long life. The cake is sliced and distributed amongst the guests.

CELEBRATION CAKE

What you need

- 275g sultanas
- 250g currants
- 250g raisins
- 110g cherries
- 75g mixed peel
- 75g ground almonds
- grated rind of one lemon
- 225g self raising flour
- 200g butter
- 200g soft brown sugar
- 4 large eggs
- 4 drops vanilla essence
- 2 tablespoons freshly squeezed lemon or orange juice
- 2 teaspoons mixed spice
- marzipan
- icing sugar
- beaten egg white
- cake board or large plate

What you do

1. Heat the oven to Gas Mark 4 or 180oC.

2. Cut the cherries and cover them with some of the flour: this will ensure they are evenly dispersed through the mixture when they are added to it.

3. Cream together the butter and sugar.

4. Sieve together the spice and flour.

5. Beat the eggs.

6. Add a little flour and a little of the egg mixture to the butter and sugar mixture and stir in thoroughly. Repeat, adding a little more egg and flour at intervals, until all is mixed together.

7. Gradually add the other ingredients to the bowl, stirring thoroughly.

8. Grease a cake tin (22-25cm in diameter) and line it with greaseproof paper and grease again.

9. Spoon in the mixture.

10. Bake for 30 minutes, then reduce the heat and cook for a further 2 1/2-3 hours, testing with a skewer after 21/2 hours.

11. Allow the cake to cool thoroughly, maybe overnight. Then store for several days in an airtight container.

12. Cover the cake on the top and sides with a thin layer of marzipan and leave for several days.

13. Mix some icing sugar with beaten egg white to make royal icing and spread on to the top and sides of the cake with a palette knife. Further icing can be piped around the edge of the cake using a piping bag and nozzle.

Note on decoration

Decorations for the cake, cake boards, piping bags and other similar items can be found in most cake shops, bakery shops and some stationers throughout the country. Some suggestions for the decoration of a Christmas cake, wedding cake or Christening cake are given below; other ideas can be found in books, magazines and photographs. Ask colleagues and children to help you collect cake decorations and ideas. Experiment and above all have fun!

Christmas Cake

Christmas cakes may be decorated with small models of robins, Christmas trees, Santa Claus, reindeer and other symbols of Christmas – which are often used by Christians even though they have no religious significance. Encircle the cake with a red, green or gold frill.

Wedding Cake

A wedding cake is usually in three tiers with the largest cake at the base and the smallest on top. The tiers may be separated by little pillars. After decorating, flowers made of icing or silk may be used to edge the top of each cake. Other emblems of marriage, such as horseshoes, bells and figures of the bridal couple, are also common.

Christening Cake

This is decorated with symbols of babyhood, such as a crib made of icing sugar. The name of the child may be written on the cake in coloured icing and a co-ordinating frill might be fastened around the cake.

5. BOOKS

'THE HOLY BIBLE'

God loves you all so much that he has given you his own son. If you believe in him, you will be blessed and live for ever.

I want you to love everyone as I have loved you.

I am the Good Shepherd. Those who follow me are my flock. They know me and they trust me. I lead them and protect them. I am ready to die for them.

If you love me with all your heart, you will join me one day in paradise.

It is easier for a camel to go through the eye of a needle than for a wicked person to go to heaven.

If you do something wrong but are sorry, I will forgive you and love you still.

I am the Light of the World.

You were like a wandering sheep, lost in the hills. I found you and brought you safely home.

Do not be afraid for I am always with you. Come, follow me. I shall be your friend.

Look at the birds, flying in the sky! My father feeds them and takes good care of them. He will do the same for you.

All of you who love me are part of God's family. We are all brothers and sisters.

I am the Bread of Life. If you believe in me, you will not go hungry.

Look how beautiful the lilies are, growing in the field. My father has cared for them and he will care for you.

Let the children come to me. Anyone who wants to go into God's house must come to him like a little child.

I was hungry and you gave me food. I was thirsty and you gave me drink. I was ill and you took care of me. Look after everyone as I look after you.

I want you to love God with all your heart, and give your life to him.

You are a little seed. I will help you to grow strong, in love for me. The birds will sing out among your branches.

I gave my life for you. If you remember this, I will always be at your side.

If you gather together to speak to me, I will be there with you.

I leave you with peace. The world cannot give peace. Take it and pass it on to everyone. Then everyone will know you are my friends.

PRAYER BOOK

Note: A6 size (quarter of A4) is recommended for the prayer book.

Morning Prayer
Morning has broken,
Like the first morning.
Blackbird has spoken,
Like the first bird.
Praise for the singing,
Praise for the morning,
Praise for them springing,
Fresh from the word.

Paternoster

Our Father, who is in heaven, holy is your name. Your kingdom come, your will be done, on earth as it is in heaven. Give us today our daily bread and forgive us what we do wrong as we forgive people who do wrong things to us. Do not let us want to do wrong and keep us away from anything bad. Amen.

Ave Maria

Hail Mary, full of grace, the Lord is with you. You are blessed among women and your child, Jesus, is blessed. Holy Mary, mother of God, pray for us because we have done wrong, now and when we die. Amen.

The Gloria

Glory to the Father and to the Son and to the Holy Spirit, as it was in the beginning, is now and ever shall be, in the world without end. Amen.

Prayer of St. Therese of Lisieux

Jesus, I love you very much. If I have you, what else do I need? All I ask is to do whatever will make you happy. Amen

Prayer of St. Patrick

Christ be with me,
Christ beside me,
Christ take care of me,
Christ comfort me.
Amen.

Prayer of St. Francis of Assisi

Jesus,
help me to bring your peace to everyone...
To bring love where there is hate...
To forgive people who have been unkind...
To bring together people who are arguing...
To tell the truth when others tell lies...
To believe in you when others do not...
To be hopeful when others give up...
To bring light wherever there is darkness...
To bring happiness wherever there is
sadness...
Jesus,
I will comfort others,
I will love others,
I will understand others.
In making others happy,
I will become closer to you
and happier in myself.
Amen.

Prayer of St. Richard of Chichester

Thank you, Jesus, for everything you have given me, for comforting me when others are unkind to me.
Jesus, my brother and my friend,
help me to know you more clearly,
to love you more dearly
and to follow you more nearly
day by day.
Amen.

Prayer of Dame Julian of Norwich

Jesus, come to me.
Be with me in all my troubles.
Keep me safe and all will be well.
Amen.

Prayer of St. Catherine of Sienna

Jesus, do not leave me
when I am in trouble for I will never leave you.
Amen.

Evening Prayer

Lord, keep us safe this night,
safe from all our fears.
May angels guard us when we sleep
Till morning light appears.

Chapter 4 **BEING IN A HINDU HOME**

The Hindu home is a celebration of the senses. On entering, the first sense to be stimulated is often that of smell – the aroma of spices in cooking, of incense burning for worship or of perfumed oil for anointing the body.

The most significant 'sight' is that of the murti (divine image) or murtis. It is in front of the murti that puja (worship) is offered and the items that are used for puja remain before the murti, resembling a shrine. Some murtis are placed within a housing that represents a temple. Murtis usually live in one of the main rooms of the home, most commonly in the kitchen near everyday objects: this positioning of the murti symbolises the presence of God in the midst of life. Hindus greet the murti by placing the palms of their hands together, pointing upwards and slightly outwards. They greet people in the same way, thus acknowledging the divinity in those they meet: the words spoken on greeting are 'Namaste' – 'Honour to you'.

The flavour of food is not only distinctive of the region from which the family originated but also appropriate to a particular time, such as a season or festival, or an occasion or period in an individual's life. For example, there are special dishes for nursing mothers. Traditionally food in a Hindu home is vegetarian because of the principle of ahimsa (harmlessness) but some Hindus eat meat apart from beef. Hindu cuisine is very nutritious and dietary laws are based on

the ethical and spiritual principles of the ancient scriptures known as the Vedas. Observant Hindus do not taste food while they are cooking it because it may not be eaten until it has first been offered to the murti. At certain times, there are days of fasting and some Hindus have individual days of fast on a regular basis.

Purity is important in a Hindu home and this is expressed in a range of ways, including personal hygiene and domestic cleanliness. For example, food except that which is very runny, is traditionally taken and eaten without cutlery: it is offensive to take food from the serving dish and eat it (that is, put it in the mouth) with the same hand; this principle applies even when cutlery is used. Many Hindus do not wear outdoor shoes indoors, especially in the kitchen: this is because they are in the presence of the murti and because shoes are dirty and 'contaminate' the home.

Hindu homes often buzz with sound, especially the sound of the human voice – both spoken and sung. The painstaking preparation of food is often undertaken by several family members, mostly women and girls, and is accompanied by conversation, story-telling and story-singing. Few Hindu homes contain copies of the scriptures but the key messages are well known and the stories they contain are recited often. Most Hindus cannot read Sanskrit, the classical language of their scriptures. The biggest single language group of British Hindus, whether

originating from India or from east Africa, is Gujarati, a language spoken in western India.

While many decisions are taken by the father or other men in the family, it is undoubtedly the mother who is the key player in family life with a strong nurturing and educating role. All the Hindus interviewed by the 'Home Team' spoke of the big-ness of small things in a Hindu home, the eternal significance of the everyday: in particular, they recalled the mother's part in ensuring that religious duties are performed, that the 'truths of the heart' are transmitted through traditional story and song, that things run smoothly, that relationships are harmonious and that life itself is kept in good repair.

The Hindu family is typically 'extended' and in India, for example, three or more generations may live together or very close by, with the result that a Hindu household is quite large. In Britain, patterns of migration and settlement have altered the nature of the extended family and children may grow up without daily contact with their grand-parents. Nevertheless it is unheard of for elderly people to live alone. As well as strong 'vertical' relationships, there are clear and significant 'horizontal' relationships – between siblings, cousins and siblings-in-law. Indian languages are rich in vocabulary to describe familial relationship and there are, for example, special forms of address for 'elder sister' and 'elder brother'. Terminology is also well defined and specific and there are, for example, different terms for maternal aunt and paternal aunt; for a brother-in-law who is one's husband's brother and a brother-in-law who is one's sister's husband.

The Hindu tradition is the oldest of the living traditions, has no 'founder' and takes many forms: it is best understood as a group of closely connected religious traditions rather than as a single religion. Most Indians live in villages and many villages or clusters of villages have their own distinctive religious practices.

Most Hindus are monotheists (believers in one God) although it may appear to outsiders that they are polytheists (believers in more than one god): most Hindus believe that God may take many forms and Hindu communities may be devotees of God in one particular form or several forms. Murtis are images of the divine and are a focus for worship, a means through which God may be approached: they are not worshipped in themselves. The English term 'idol' is therefore misleading and its negative 'pagan' connotations are offensive to many Hindus. Most Hindus in Britain are Vaishnavas, devotees of Vishnu who is believed to have ten avatars (incarnations) – the most well known of whom are Rama and Krishna. Many stories about the lives of Rama and Krishna are recorded in Hindu scriptures and are passed from one generation to the next through the tradition of story-telling in words, music and dance.

Most Hindus believe that all forms of life are connected and that the individual soul passes from one form to another in a succession of lives, through the cycle of life, death and rebirth. A person's actions in a lifetime determine the form or state into which the soul is reborn: this ethical principle is known as karma and is the central concept underlying the traditional caste system which has four varnas (main social levels). In one sense, the system is a way of describing human inequalities and, in another sense, it is a way of explaining the need for personal development and improvement. Westerners, including European missionaries and imperialists, have typically been critical of the caste system, often without understanding its nature and purpose or its place in Hindu thought as a whole. Some Indians themselves have also sought to abolish or amend the caste system, for example, Guru Nanak (the founder of the Sikh tradition), a number of Hindu reformers in the 19th and 20th centuries and, perhaps most famously, Mahatma Gandhi. The caste system remains an area of sensitivity for many Hindus.

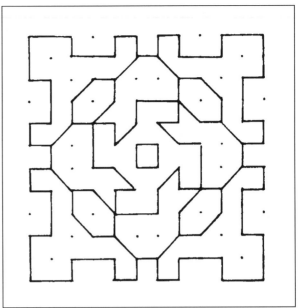

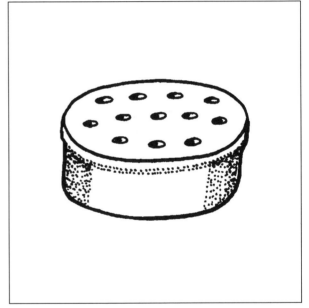

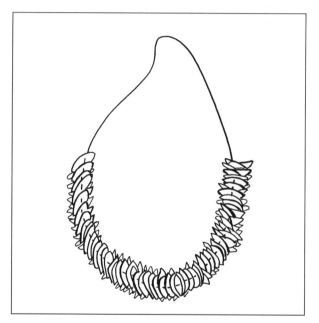

2. 'DOORWAYS' TO A HINDU HOME

COLOUR AND LIGHT
specific to Hinduism

English
- colour and shade vocabulary
- colour symbolism
- stories and poems about colours
- writing Rama and Sita play
- retelling story individually and in groups

Mathematics
- multiples and one-to-one
- correspondence on Ravana's head(s)
- measuring time through candle clocks
- measuring temperature
- hue sequencing
- matching and sorting colours and lights

Science
- types of light sources e.g. torches and candles
- safety with fire
- heat and temperature
- light circuits
- human eye
- 3 requirements for fire: heat, fuel, oxygen
- inverted images
- shadows and silhouettes
- refraction and rainbow prisms

Technology
- making pin-hole cameras
- designing and making diwas and other candle-holders
- making colour games

History
- story of light from early fire-making to electricity
- events involving fire such as the Great Fire of London

Geography
- sun, moon and stars, day and night
- eclipses
- Aurora Borealis
- forest fires
- comparisons and contrasts between Britain and India

Art
- rangoli patterns
- writing with magic pens
- making Diwali cards
- 'hot' and 'cold' colours
- colour mixing
- primary, secondary and tertiary colours
- creating pictures to evoke light and fire
- appreciation of light in painting
- 'playing' with light and colour such as through marbling and bubbling

Music
- listening to and recreating Indian music
- singing songs on the theme of light and colour

Physical education
- traffic light games

Religious education
- puja
- colour symbolism
- light/dark symbolism
- use of light in ritual and custom
- Diwali and Holi
- story of Ramayana
- visit to mandir

CLOTHES
generic but with emphasis on Hinduism

English
- ❏ vocabulary of body parts
- ❏ vocabulary of clothing and characteristics of fabrics
- ❏ types of clothing
- ❏ reading and writing stories about clothing
- ❏ creating slogans for T-shirts
- ❏ discussion of gender factors in clothing

Mathematics
- ❏ geometric and other patterns on fabrics
- ❏ counting stitches and clothing
- ❏ accessories such as buttons
- ❏ graphs of clothing sizes

Science
- ❏ sorting fabrics into types, including natural and synthetic
- ❏ warm/cool fabrics
- ❏ dyes and stain removers, natural and synthetic
- ❏ durability, absorbency and fading experiments with fabrics
- ❏ laundering and dry-cleaning

Technology
- ❏ designing and making clothes for children and dolls
- ❏ creating fabrics by knitting and weaving

History
- ❏ old clothes or pictures of them
- ❏ time line of clothes fashions through the ages

Geography
- ❏ clothing around the world, including economic and climatic factors
- ❏ discussion of cultural and socio-economic factors related to clothes worn in Britain

Art
- ❏ making cut-out dolls
- ❏ clothes designs and patterns
- ❏ creating collages of fabrics
- ❏ printing, painting and embroidering fabric
- ❏ images of clothing in the media, especially bill boards and magazines

Music
- ❏ creating dressing sequence songs
- ❏ folk songs about fabric making e.g. 19th century English mill songs

Physical education
- ❏ Indian dancing
- ❏ miming wearing different types of clothing e.g. armour

Religious education
- ❏ clothing for religious ceremonies
- ❏ clothing always worn as sign of cultural identity or religious commitment
- ❏ significance of colours in various traditions e.g. red for weddings and white for mourning in the Hindu tradition

3.'FURNISHINGS'

TOE'RAM

(welcome frieze hung over doorway)

What you need

- template of rangoli motif
- thick card
- coloured shiny paper
- string
- 50cm length of tinsel
- glitter
- varied small shiny objects, such as sequins, bright buttons or beads
- strong stapler
- PVA
- large drawing pins
- 'jester' bells (optional)
- if available, a small murti (image of deity), such as sticker or cut-out picture: Lord Ganesha is particularly welcoming.

What you do

1. Using template, cut out odd number of shapes in card: seven is probably enough for a home-corner entrance.

2. Cut out the same number of shapes in shiny paper: if using several colours, keep a symmetrical arrangement in mind. Turn the template over and cut the same number in the same colours of shiny paper.

3. Stick the shiny paper pieces on both sides of the card shapes.

4. Stick the shiny objects on the shapes – on one side only – creating rangoli or circular patterns on each one, and an overall symmetrical arrangement. If using a murti, stick in on the middle one. If using bells, attach to bottom of shapes.

5. Fold over top of each shape and staple, allowing a gap through which to pass string.

6. Attach tinsel to front, covering staples and join on to string at each end.

7. Fix completed toe'ram to home-corner entrance by winding ends of string round drawing pins.

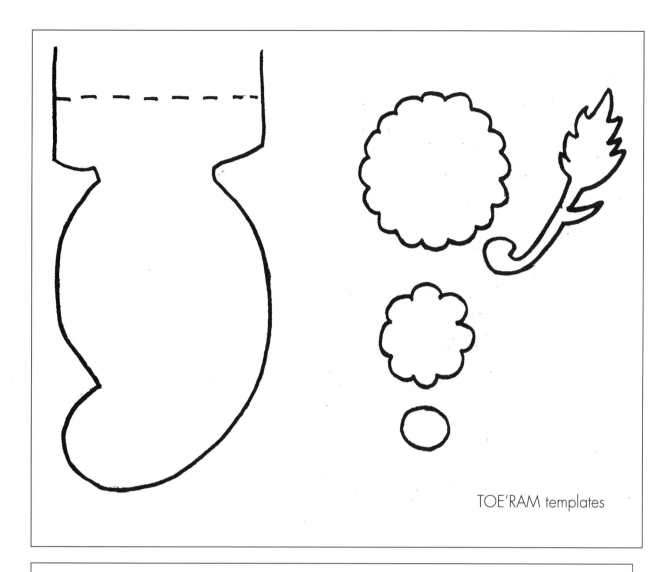

TOE'RAM templates

DIWA
(light dish)

Diwas are usually made of clay or metal. A
night light (small candle in a metal dish) may
be substituted but this diwa emulates
terracotta and is satisfying for children to
make themselves.

What you need
- brown plasticine (about the size of a
  walnut)
- round wick or, if not available, a piece of
  cotton wool (about the size of a large
  peanut)
- ghee (clarified butter) or olive oil

What you do
1. Roll the plasticine into a ball and mould
   it into a thumb-pot about 3-4 cm in
   diameter. Flatten the bottom so that the
   pot stands up unaided! Pinching one side
   of the pot to form a lip will give an
   authentic look to the diwa.

2. If using cotton wool for the wick, twist it
   to form a point. Soak the wick in ghee or
   oil, place it in the centre of the diwa and
   light. If children are using the diwa
   without direct adult supervision,
   substitute scraps of yellow or orange
   tissue paper to create a 'lighted' wick.

RANGOLI MAT

(patterned welcome mat)

Rangoli mats are symmetrical and may be designed from any geometric, leafy or floral shape. In some communities, the authentic motif is a mango. The patterns may be used as a basis for the design or the children may create their own.

What you need

- either sheets of tissue paper in an assortment of colours or a selection of legumes such as lentils (orange, brown and green), rice, seeds and dried beans or powder paints in varied colours

- sheet of sugar paper or A3 card

- clear plastic bag or sheeting to fit over sugar paper/card

What you do

1. Sketch the design on to the sugar paper or card and decide which colours and materials to use in each section.

2. Spread glue on one section and fill the area with scrunched tissue or legumes, or sprinkle with powder paint (blow powder paint off other areas!) Repeat for other sections until mat is covered.

3. When the mat is thoroughly dry, protect it by covering it with plastic.

4. Tape it to floor outside the door of home.

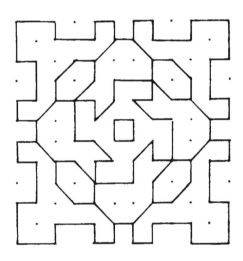

PUJA TRAY

(tray holding items used in worship)

The five elements are involved in puja as offerings to the deity: earth (represented by something grown, usually fruit); fire (a light burning); air (incense); water; and ether (symbolised by the sound of a bell).

What you need for tray, fruit dish, bell and water container

- newspaper and paste or 'instant' papier maché.
- lid of a round biscuit/sweet tin (about 15-20cm in diameter)
- lid of a jar or tin (about 6cm in diameter)
- one section from a plastic egg box
- 10cm doweling, about the thickness of a match
- strong glue
- strong thread
- 'jester' bell
- plastic 35mm cylindrical film case, without lid
- small metal or plastic spoon, such that comes with individual ice cream tub
- gold spray paint

What you do: tray, fruit dish and water container

1. With papier maché, cover all surfaces of the large lid, the small lid, the egg box section and, if plastic, the spoon; cover the outer surfaces only of the film box. Leave to dry thoroughly.

2. Spray with gold paint all surfaces covered with papier maché. Leave to dry thoroughly again.

What you do: puja bell

1. Pierce a hole in one end of the doweling and attach the bell firmly.

2. Pierce a hole in the egg box section and push the opposite end of the doweling through so that the bell nestles inside the egg box section. Check that the bell has room to ring!

3. Using a small amount of glue, secure the doweling to the outside of the egg box section.

JOSS STICK HOLDER

(incense holder)

What you need
- top of plastic drum containing pepper or spices
- small lump of plasticine
- short incense sticks

What you do
1. Carefully enlarge holes in top of drum, using fine skewer or other sharp instrument.

2. Press plasticine inside top of drum.

3. Push incense sticks through holes and into the plasticine.

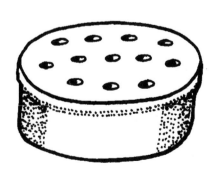

MURTI

(image of deity)

Moulded brass murtis, about 6-8cm high, can be obtained from shops selling Hindu artefacts: they will have greater definition if they are painted in bright colours, using enamels (such as lead-free car re-touch paints). Use a picture of the appropriate murti as a guide to colours. Murtis can also be made by mounting and framing Hindu stickers. If neither brass murtis nor stickers are available, the templates given are a good substitute.

Murti of Krishna

Murti of Saraswati

What you need
- picture of Krishna, Rama and Sita, Ganesha or Sarasvati
- clear contact film
- coloured or gold card
- short piece of string or cord (optional)
- sequins or glitter (optional)
- PVA

What you do

1. Reduced the picture on photocopier to keep the size of the murti in proportion.

2. Colour picture vividly and cover with contact film.

3. Create a frame by mounting picture on slightly larger piece of coloured or gold card.

4. Decorate frame with sequins or glitter, if liked.

5. Prop up the murti, as the focus of the shrine, against a wall or attach a loop to the back of the murti and hang it on the wall.

6. Arrange the puja tray in front of the murti.

Murti of Ganesha

Murti of Rama and Sita

MURTI HAAR

(flower garland for image of deity)

What you need

- strong thread
- flower petals, fresh or cut from coloured tissue paper, about 1cm in length
- small leaves, fresh or cut from green tissue paper, about 1cm in length

What you do

1. Thread a needle and knot the end.

2. Thread petals and leaves alternately until the desired length is achieved.

3. Tie the two ends together firmly.

4. If using a brass murti, drape the haar round the neck of the murti and 'skim' the base at the front. If using a picture, fix the murti to the corners on the wrong side, using a small piece of masking tape.

HAAR

(flower garland)

What you need

- 20 large circles (approximately 12cm diameter) and 20 small circles (approximately 8cm in diameter) of tissue paper in assorted colours; these can be purchased through craft suppliers or cut by hand from sheets and scraps

- straws (drinking or art) cut into 20 x 3cm lengths

- 140cm strong embroidery thread

- thick blunt-ended needle

What you do

1. Tie a length of straw to the end of the thread.

2. Place a small tissue circle on a large tissue circle of contrasting colour and pinch them together in the centre to form a flower.

3. Stitch the flower firmly to the end of the length of straw.

4. Thread another length of straw and repeat flower process.

5. Continue alternating flowers and straws until all are used.

6. Tie off end of thread through first length of straw, making a circular garland.

SARI

An authentic sari is difficult for a 'waist-less' child to keep on when moving freely. This garment is a look-alike sari, worn like a wrap-over skirt, with an extended length for draping over shoulders and head.

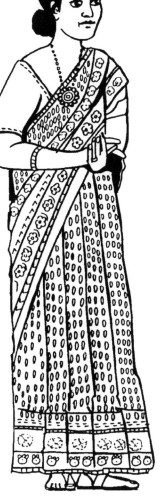

What you need

- 3m x 70cm fine soft fabric, such as voile or chiffon, in light or bright colours, either patterned or plain with border design for bottom edge of sari. An old sari, if available, is ideal and will give enough fabric for two child-sized saris

- 10cm strip Velcro (doubled-sided)

- sewing thread

What you do

1. Hem all raw edges.

2. With the right side of fabric uppermost, mark accurately the following measurements from the left-hand side of the longside: 70cm (A), 90cm (B), 110cm (C), 130cm (D), 150cm (E).

3. Bring point A over to point B to form a pleat and pin.

4. Continue making pleats by bringing point B over to point C, point C over to point D and point D over to point E. This makes four pleats, one on top of the other.

5. Stitch down very firmly.

6. Attach one side of Velcro strip underneath the pleats on the wrong side. Attach the other side of the Velcro strip on the right side at the left-hand edge.

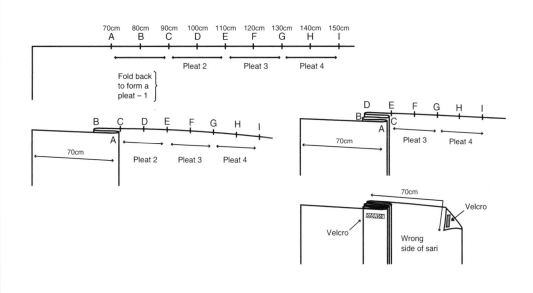

KURTA

(boy's suit)

This is a fairly traditional suit worn by men and sometimes by boys – of all religious traditions – in the Indian subcontinent and sometimes in Britain on formal or religious occasions.

Note
- This outfit has set sleeves and neck facings: it can only be made by someone who has basic dressmaking skills.

What you need
- 1.5m light coloured polyester/cotton fabric
- matching sewing thread
- matching embroidery thread
- 3 small matching buttons
- 50cm narrow elastic

What you do
1. Using patterns, cut all pieces from fabric. Refer to picture detail when making up the garments. Allow a 1cm seam and neaten edges.

2. Use left over pieces of fabric to cut strips to bind neck, and top and bottom facings for neck opening. Make button holes and attach buttons. If it is not possible to do these, a similar effect can be achieved by sewing buttons on the top facing of the neck opening and poppers between the top and bottom facings. Finish front of top by embroidering flowers in daisy stitch.

3. On wrong side of trousers, turn top over 1cm and turn over again. Machine firmly, leaving a small opening to pass elastic. Thread elastic through, adjusting to size required. Secure elastic with strong stitches.

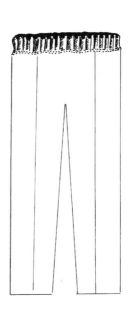

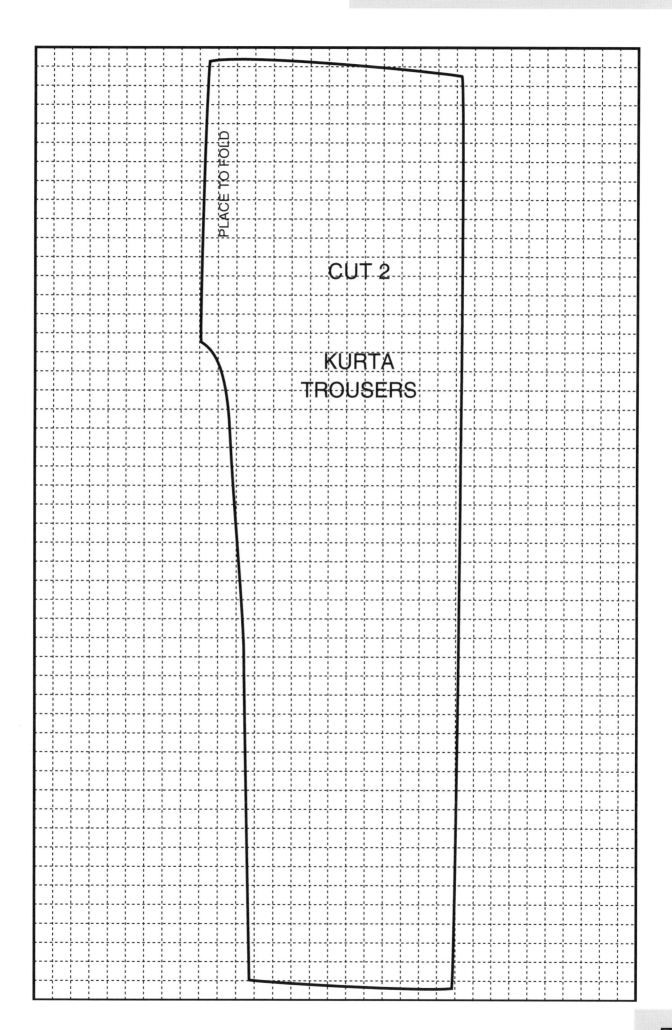

PLACE TO FOLD

CUT 2

KURTA
TROUSERS

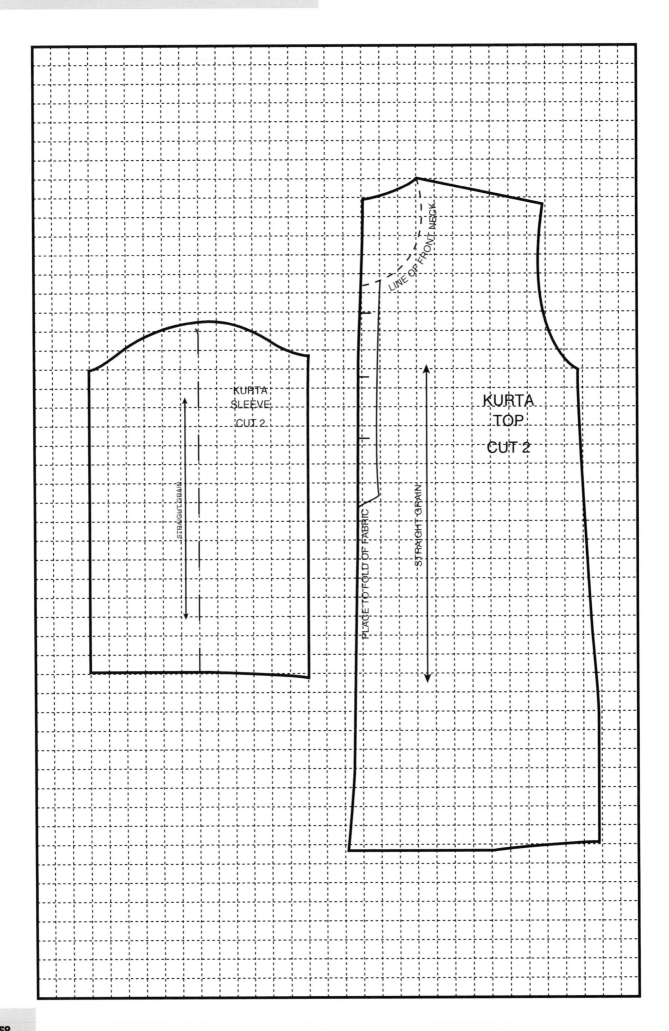

KURTA
SLEEVE
CUT 2

STRAIGHT GRAIN

LINE OF FRONT NECK

PLACE TO FOLD OF FABRIC

KURTA
TOP
CUT 2

STRAIGHT GRAIN

4. Food

CHAPATI

In the north of India wheat is a staple food and many dishes are served with bread, such as chapatis. This recipe makes about 15 chapatis.

What you need

- 250g sieved wheatmeal or wholemeal flour, plus extra for dusting
- 175ml water
- a little vegetable oil to grease pan

What you do

1. Put the flour into a bowl. Slowly add the water, gathering the flour together to form a soft dough.

2. Knead the dough for 6-8 minutes or until it is smooth.

3. Put the dough in a bowl, cover with a damp cloth and leave for half an hour.

4. Set an Indian tava or any other cast iron frying pan to heat over a medium low flame for 10 minutes. When it is very hot, turn the heat to low.

5. Knead the dough again and divide into 15 (roughly). Dust hands with flour as the dough may be sticky.

6. Take one part of the dough and form a ball.

7. Flour the work surface and press the ball down to make a patty.

8. Roll the patty out until it is about 15cm in diameter. Pick up the chappati and pat in your hands to shake off the extra flour. Then slap it onto the hot pan.

9. Let it cook on a low heat for about a minute and turn it over. Take the pan off the stove and put the chappati directly on the top of the low flame: it should puff up!

10. Repeat with the remaining balls.

Note

- The pan and the cooked chapatis are very hot and children should not be directly involved at these stages.

- Ideally, chapatis should be eaten as soon as they are made but they may be wrapped in foil and stored in the fridge for up to a day and then frozen. They can then be reheated (still in the foil) at Gas mark 7 or 425°F for 15-20 minutes.

PAKORAS

These tasty snacks are delicious on their own or can be served to accompany a variety of savoury dishes, whether meat-based or vegetarian.

What you need
- 225g plain flour
- pinch of baking powder
- 1 teaspoon salt
- 1/2 teaspoon each of coriander, red chilli, ground ginger
- pinch of ground cummin
- water
- oil for deep frying
- vegetables (potatoes, spinach or aubergines, finely chopped)

What you do
1. Sieve all the spices, baking powder and flour, and mix in a large bowl.
2. Add enough water to make a thick batter, and mix well.
3. Add the vegetables to the mixture.
4. Heat some oil in a large pan until hot.
5. Drop the mixture into the oil (about a dessert spoonful at a time).
6. When golden brown, remove, drain and serve at once.

Note
Frying the pakoras should only be done by adults.

KULFI

This is an extremely popular ice-cream dessert, which is firm in texture. It makes a refreshing end to any meal.

What you need
- 150ml milk
- 2 tablespoons ground rice
- 1 tablespoon ground almonds
- 450ml evaporated milk
- 1 level teaspoon ground cardamom
- 50g sugar
- 450ml double cream
- 1 tablespoon rose water or vanilla essence
- 25g unsalted pistachio nuts, lightly crushed

What you do
1. Warm the milk.
2. Put the rice and almonds into a bowl.
3. Add the warm milk, little by little, to make a thin paste which can be poured.
4. Stir continuously, breaking up any lumps. Sieve if necessary.
5. Heat the evaporated milk until it is at boiling point.
6. Add the cardamom to the evaporated milk.
7. Remove the pan from the heat.
8. Add the almond, rice and milk mixture. Stir continuously.
9. Add the sugar and cream.
10. Place the pan over medium heat to cook for 12-15 minutes. Continue stirring.
11. Add the rosewater or vanilla essence and half the pistachio nuts, and mix well.
12. Mix well. Allow to cool, stirring to prevent a skin forming.
13. Place the mixture in a plastic container or divide it between several yogurt pots.
14. Top with the remaining nuts and freeze for 4-5 hours.
15. Before serving, place the kulfi in the refrigerator for 11/2 – 13/4 hours to soften it.
16. Remove from moulds and serve.

5. BOOKS

EXTRACTS FROM THE BHAVAGAD GITA

Sometimes you need to give things up to help people and to please God.

Give things up because your heart says so, not because you want a reward.

Read words that are peaceful and beautiful. The Holy books have peaceful and beautiful words in them.

Find light inside you and be with God.

Love me because you are dear to me.

Whoever you worship, if you love them, you love God.

When you are peaceful you are with God. You are with God when you are happy or sad, pleased or cross, praised or told off.

Think of God when you work. Do your work peacefully and not because you want a reward.

God will give to you if you are peaceful with yourself and other people.

Be peaceful to everyone, even people you don't like and those who are horrid to you.

Want things that are good and that help people.

Do not be greedy. If you are greedy you will find it hard to see God.

You will be happy if you work peacefully.

If you would like to be like those in Heaven, be kind and gentle, find good things in people and forgive them, tell the truth and have lots of energy.

Do not be greedy. Be happy with what you have.

Love all living things the same amount. Love a holy person or an animal like a friend.

Find things inside you that make you glad.

Be peaceful, not angry.

Be peaceful and pure, like God is.

Do not be jealous. Be glad with what you have.

Chapter 5 **BEING IN A JEWISH HOME**

The home is the heart of Jewish life and plays a much more significant part in the development of Jewish children's identity and commitment than the synagogue. Both the synagogue and the home are heirs to rituals from the ancient Jewish temple but it is in family life that these are nurtured in concrete ways. Community life based in the synagogue is not an optional extra and plays its part in the development of spiritual sensitivity and ethical awareness but the major responsibility for the education and religious socialisation of Jewish children traditionally belongs to the parents – not to teachers and rabbis. Every single aspect of Jewish life is celebrated and commemorated at home – often to a much larger extent than the synagogue.

In Orthodox communities, the roles and responsibilities of men and women are 'equal but different': equal in value but different in character. Men play the prominent role in public worship, leading prayers and chanting from the Torah while women's major responsibilities are to the family: they have the duty and privilege of nurturing and religiously educating the children, in creating a Jewish atmosphere that is both devout and vibrant, and in ensuring that the home is kosher (fit and proper) in matters of food and dress, hygiene, study and prayer. It is often the women who play the greater part in those activities which sustain the community and meet other people's needs, such as by visiting the sick and initiating or supporting charitable concerns. Financial and domestic tasks are undertaken by both men and women, especially those involved in preparing

for Shabbat (the weekly Sabbath), Pesach (the spring festival of Passover) and Sukkot (the autumn festival of tabernacles). Jewish women are not debarred from pursuing a career and for centuries have been encouraged to follow their vocational interests: in some ultra-Orthodox families women may be proud to run the home and, by having a full-time job, to support the family financially so that their husbands can pursue extended full-time religious study. In progressive communities, the roles and responsibilities of men and women are 'equal and similar': equal in value and increasingly interchangeable. In the 20th century, especially in recent decades, the roles and responsibilities of men and women are shifting in emphasis in progressive and some Orthodox communities.

The Jewish tradition has been matrilineal since ancient times, that is, Jewish identity and status are passed from mother to children. While it is possible to convert to Judaism, the majority of Jews are people born of a Jewish mother. A child's matrilineal identity and status are complemented by their Hebrew name being linked to their father: an orthodox child's name is 'X son/daughter of father's name'; a progressive child's name is 'X son/daughter of father's name and mother's name'.

Daily life in an observant Jewish home is punctuated with experiences and objects which heighten devotion to God, enhance ethical awareness and strengthen family and community ties. The Jewish day is shaped by three times for 'public' prayer, as well as

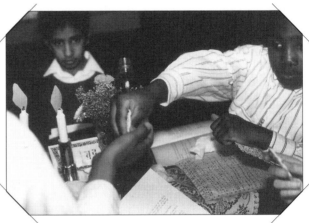

personal prayers and devotions on going to bed and getting up. There are blessings for various kinds of food and for other actions and experiences, such as seeing something beautiful or fulfilling a commandment. It is perhaps at the family table – whether for eating or studying or both – that the significance of the home is most clear: several of the Jews interviewed by the 'Home Team' unpacked the idea of the home as a little temple, with the table as the altar and the parents as the priests.

Judaism, in its earliest forms, dates back about 4000 years but is continually evolving. It has no specific 'founder' but the Jewish people originated or emerged in and around the Land of Israel and twice in ancient times Jews were taken or driven into exile from their homeland. Homeland and dispersion, exile and return, persecution and survival are significant themes in Jewish life and thought. This well-established pattern of settlement has resulted in the prevailing culture influencing much of Jewish lifestyle so that, for example, the majority of Jews speak the vernacular at home.

Broadly there are two main cultural groups: Sefardi communities originating in the southern Europe, north Africa and Arab lands, and Ashkenazi communities originating in northern and eastern Europe. For centuries, Sefardi Jews spoke Ladino, a language based on medieval Spanish but very small numbers speak it today; Ashkenazi Jews spoke Yiddish, a language based on medieval German but written in Hebrew script and, although the bulk of Yiddish speaking communities were exterminated by the Nazis, there are some Jews who still speak Yiddish today. The differences between Sefardi and Ashkenazi cultures are fairly superficial: the pronunciation of Hebrew, food preferences, names and, in some respect, prayer customs. World-wide there are more Sefardi than Ashkenazi Jews and the differential is increasing this is especially noticeable today in the State of Israel. In the 17th century Oliver Cromwell expressly invited Sefardi Jews to 'return' to England. Askenazi Jews came to Britain as refugees mainly from Poland and Russia at the end of the 19th century and from Germany in the 1930s. There are more Ashkenazi than Sefardi Jews in Britain today and, where there are cultural differences, it is Askhenazi culture which colours the rituals and artefacts in *Homing In*.

Jews have traditionally been sustained by strong family ties and community involvement. Numerically the Jewish people is small but, especially in the modern period when they have been able to participate in the 'open society', they have been very much in evidence in cultural life. There are Jewish communities throughout the world but most are found in Israel, North America and Europe, including countries of the former Soviet Union. Jewish individuals and communities and the State of Israel are often in the news and media coverage may be a useful topical resource for older pupils but they should be alerted to the anti-semitic bias which much of it contains.

It is misleading to speak of the 'Jewish race' as Jews may belong to any ethnic group and it is more accurate to speak of 'the Jewish people'. For some Jews, being Jewish is less a matter of 'religion' than of cultural identity and, especially in Israel and North America, there are small but significant numbers of secular Jews. Within the British Jewish community, the affectionate and humourous term 'cardiac Jews' has been coined for those who consider themselves to be 'Jewish at heart'! The majority of Jews, nevertheless, have been described as 'ethical monotheists' – believers in on God and followers of a tradition that emphasises socially responsive actions.

It may be tempting to draw comparisons between Judaism and Christianity because of Christianity's roots in ancient Judaism – and, for example, to use the term 'Old Testament' when referring to the Jewish/Hebrew Bible. However, while it may be helpful to understand, for example, Jesus' Jewish background or Passover as the origin of the Eucharist, it is also important to appreciate Judaism as a living religion – not merely as a precursor to Christianity – and to approach it in its own terms.

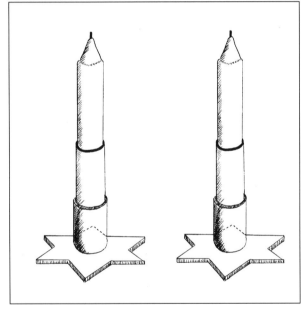

שבת שלום

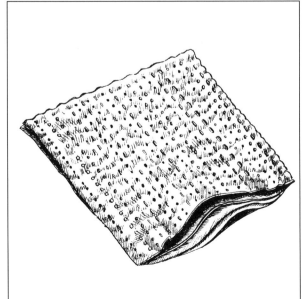

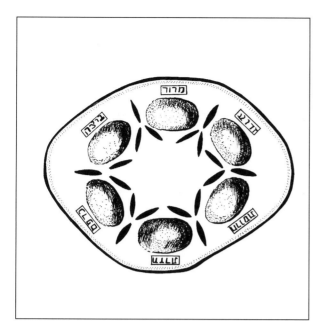

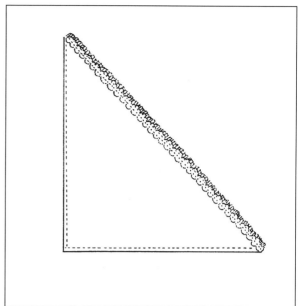

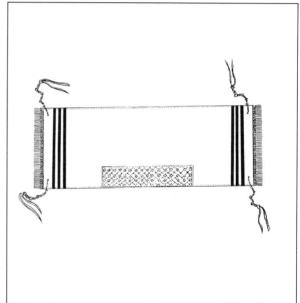

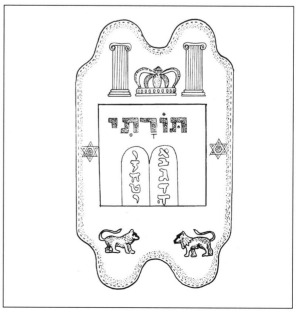

2. 'DOORWAYS' TO A JEWISH HOME

SHABBAT AND 'THE WEEK'
specific to Judaism

English
- stories from the Torah
- writing Torah pages
- making and using a siddur
- writing prayers and thanksgiving after meals
- invitations to Shabbat meal
- greetings
- 'week' word games

Mathematics
- creating a 'Star of David' inscribed in a circle
- calculating amount of food and cost of meal for family and X guests
- divisions of time (second, minute...)
- measuring time – objectively and subjectively
- making tzitzit, by carefully counting knots and 'windings', for tallit corners

Science
- experiments with the effects of various durations and intensities on bread dough, both at rising and baking stages
- sun and rain in crops production experiments with yeast
- hygiene in food preparation
- collecting and/or growing food from Israel e.g. orange seeds

Technology
- designing and making candles and candle sticks
- designing and making a mezuzah
- making appropriate games for Shabbat (that do not require breaking Shabbat e.g. writing, painting, tearing)
- researching recipes for Shabbat foods
- cooking a Shabbat meal

History
- weekly sequence of events
- creation stories

Geography
- Shabbat customs around in various Jewish communities
- Israel
- food grown according to season

Art
- paintings and other art work on theme of light
- making art straw havdalah candles
- decorating a kippah, kiddush cup, tallit bag etc. with Jewish motifs
- art work inspired by tallit stripes

Music
- songs about the week
- listening to and learning to sing Jewish songs about Shabbat

Physical education
- creating dance on the theme of work and rest

Religious education
- Shabbat meal simulation
- researching and/or interviewing Jews about the value of Shabbat
- Shabbat in the Torah

WEDDINGS
generic but with emphasis on Judaism

English
- ❏ wedding vocabulary
- ❏ wedding invitations, replies and orders of service
- ❏ composing vows and prayers
- ❏ letters to hotels and caterers etc.
- ❏ exploring images and roles in folklore on marriage/romance themes, including games and rhymes such as 'Postman's Knock', 'The farmer's in his den', 'He loves me, he loves me not', 'Tinker, tailor'...
- ❏ making books as gifts
- ❏ composing wedding sermons and speeches

Mathematics
- ❏ cost of weddings
- ❏ survey of ages of wedding couples
- ❏ computing catering needs
- ❏ shapes in hupah and synagogue design

Science
- ❏ contrasting wedding food with ordinary diet
- ❏ studies of life cycles

Technology
- ❏ cooking wedding celebration food
- ❏ making and improvising wedding garments
- ❏ designing, making and evaluating appropriate Jewish wedding gifts
- ❏ making musical instruments
- ❏ model hupah
- ❏ model synagogue

History
- ❏ family trees
- ❏ history of wedding traditions

Geography
- ❏ wedding routes
- ❏ table plans
- ❏ wedding customs around the world

Art
- ❏ Hebrew inscriptions
- ❏ creating realia for wedding souvenir book
- ❏ making place settings
- ❏ making 'pretend' candles
- ❏ designing wedding cards and invitations
- ❏ appreciating art on wedding themes

Music
- ❏ appreciating songs for weddings
- ❏ exploring imagery in popular music on wedding/romance themes

Physical education
- ❏ wedding dances

Religious education
- ❏ beliefs about marriage and wedding customs in religious traditions
- ❏ ideas of love and commitment, and individual, family and community responsibilities
- ❏ wedding stories about exemplary figures in faith traditions
- ❏ stories about marriage in faith traditions
- ❏ simulation of wedding rituals and customs
- ❏ visit to synagogue

3. 'FURNISHINGS'

MEZUZAH
(scroll box for doorpost)

What you need
- either plastic canister used for 35mm film, with lid or small (spent) roll-up paste sticks (e.g. Pritt or Uhu)
- template
- thin white or cream card

What you do
1. If using film canister, cut out template and colour buildings of Jerusalem. Wrap round film box and stick. Apply firm pressure. A circle of card may also be stuck to the lid.

2. If using roll-up paste stick, cut a piece of card to cover. Copy on to card the three Hebrew letters from picture of narrow mezuzah. Wrap round paste stick, glue and apply pressure. Cut a strip of card to stick on lid and decorate with six-pointed stars or floral motif.

3. Cut a piece of card the same size as the template. Write as beautifully as possible, 'Hear O Israel (or, people). The Lord is our God. The Lord is one.' Roll it up and slip it into the film case. Replace lid.

4. Attach to doorpost, using a hinge of masking tape.

Mezuzah, using a film canister

Mezuzah, using a paste container

Templates for mezuzah made from film cannister

Templates for mezuzah made from paste container

CANDLESTICKS

What you need

- 2 large (spent) roll-up paste sticks (e.g. Pritt or Uhu)
- 2 chubby (spent) felt tip pens, with lids
- silver or gold paper
- plasticine in neutral colour
- scraps of yellow or orange tissue paper
- thick card (optional)

What you do

1. Cover paste sticks with silver or gold paper, ensuring that the hollow is neatly finished.

2. Turn them upside-down so that the hollow is uppermost.

3. Cover felt tip pens with white paper.

4. Put a small piece of plasticine in the hollow of each paste stick and push the bottom of a felt tip pen in each.

5. To create 'flames', attach scraps of yellow or orange tissue paper to the tips of the felt tip pens.

Note

For added stability, the candles can be mounted on small stands, made from thick card cut into circular or six-pointed star shapes and covered with gold/silver paper.

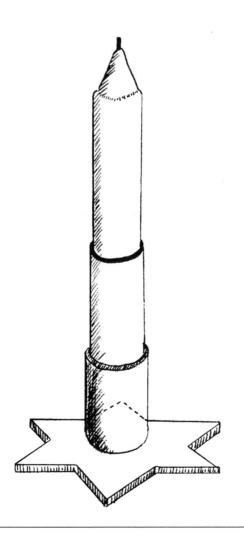

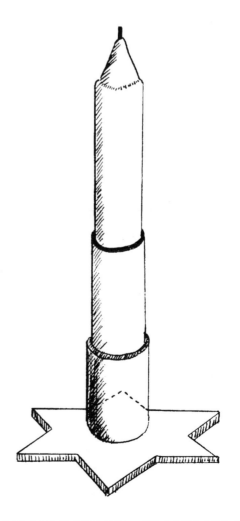

KIDDUSH CUP

(wine/grape juice cup, for sanctifying Sabbath and Festivals)

Kiddush cups come in all shapes and sizes and are usually made of silver. Sometimes they are completely unadorned but traditionally they are engraved or painted with Jewish motifs, such as those suggested.

What you need
- stainless steel egg cup
- lead-free enamel paints (such as car touch-up paints), in yellow, purple and green

What you do
1. Paint a yellow six-pointed star (Magen David – Star of David) on one side of the cup and a bunch of purple grapes, with green leaves, on the opposite side. Refer to picture for detail.

MATZA COVER

(layered cloth to hold three pieces of unleavened bread)

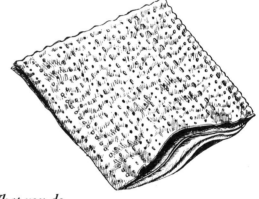

Matza is available from Jewish food shops and supermarkets in most large towns.

Traditional matzah covers are large, round or square, of silky or velvety fabric and embroidered with Passover motifs. This design departs from tradition and resembles a piece of matzah. The lines of uneven running stitches in varying shades of brown, beige and cream, are intended to resemble the 'knobbled' effect of matzah. Children who sew in crooked lines merit great praise and gain self-esteem in this activity!

What you need
- 4 pieces of felt, 20-25cm square, in 'bread' colours
- varied bread-coloured embroidery threads
- 3 pieces square matza (unleavened bread)

What you do
1. On one piece of felt only, take one colour of thread and make an irregular line of running stitches across one piece of felt, leaving a gap of 0.5cm at each end. Change colour of thread and make another line of irregular running stitches about 0.5cm parallel to the first. Continue until the felt is covered.

2. Pile the 4 pieces of felt on top of each other, with the right side of the stitched piece uppermost.

3. Join on 3 sides only with a line of running stitches about 0.5cm from the edges.

4. Place a piece of matza in each of the layers thus created.

HALLAH COVER

(cover for Sabbath Loaves)

What you need

- white or pale coloured cloth (or felt) in A4 size
- small pieces of felt in grey, yellow and browns
- 105cm fringing, preferably soft and white
- templates

What you do

1. Copy templates and cut out in felt: candle shapes in grey and yellow, cup shape in grey or yellow and several brown, round pieces for each loaf.

2. Stick pieces onto cloth, as shown in picture.

3. Trace Hebrew words ('Shabbat Shalom', meaning 'Sabbath peace') on to cloth. Outline in felt pen or embroider.

4. Stick or stitch fringing all round edges.

שבת שלום

SEDER PLATE

(plate holding symbolic foods eaten at the Seder)

This plate follows the most common conventions but there are variations. All have spaces for the shank-bone, roast egg, karpas (green vegetable such as parsley), haroset (paste resembling mortar) and maror (bitter vegetable such as horseradish). This plate has a sixth space for hazeret (another kind of bitter vegetable, such as chicory).

What you need

- photocopy of Hebrew labels
- dinner-sized unbreakable plate (such as used for picnics or in school canteen): it will be used as a mould but later redeemed from papier maché; an oval shape is best – a round plate can be made oval by adding 2 curved pieces of cardboard
- plasticine
- Vaseline or other barrier
- newspaper and paste, or instant papier maché
- gold spray
- felt tip pens
- PVA

What you do

1. Make six balls of plasticine, each the size of a walnut, and press them on to the back of the plate, spacing them evenly as shown in the diagram.

2. Grease the entire surface with Vaseline (to prevent sticking).

3. Cover with several layers of papier machÈ to achieve a smooth effect. If using newspaper, finish with a layer of white paper strips.

4. Leave to dry in a warm place for several days.

5. Carefully remove plate and plasticine, ensuring that no plasticine remains in the hollows of the 'plate' shape.

6. Apply more papier maché to other side of 'plate' shape including the hollows. When thoroughly dry, spray gold.

7. Cut out Hebrew labels. Stick in position and (if liked) decorate as shown.

8. Cover all surfaces with a thick coat of PVA glue: the Seder plate will not be completely waterproof but will be resistant to damp food and can be wiped lightly.

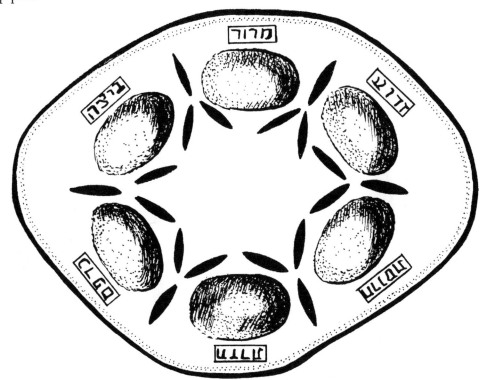

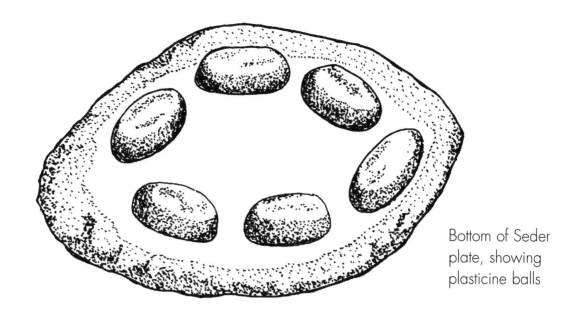

Bottom of Seder plate, showing plasticine balls

Hebrew name	Transliteration	Translation
מרור	maror	bitter vegetable e.g. horseradish
זרוע	zeroa	bone
ביצה	beytza	roasted egg
כרפס	karpas	green vegetable e.g. parsley
חזרת	hazeret	leafy bitter vegetable e.g. chicory
חרוסת	haroset	mixture resembling mortar - made of chopped / ground nuts, grated apple, honey, grape juice

Hebrew labels for Seder plate, with English transliteration and translation

KIPPAH

(skull cap worn by boys and men)

The colour of the cap is not significant but blue, black and maroon are common; they may be decorated or plain.

What you need

- template
- fabric (preferably velvety or silky) 25cm square
- lining material 25cm square
- matching thread
- button in complementary shade (optional)
- decorative embroidery thread in contrasting shade, or silver or gold (optional)

What you do

1. Photocopy template and use to cut four pieces of the velvety or silky material.

2. With right sides together and allowing a 0.5cm seam, join the pieces together along the straight edges so that the points meet and a 'cap' is formed. Repeat the process with the lining material, allowing a 0.75cm seam so that it will 'sit' easily inside the cap.

3. If decorating the velvety or silky material, embroider all panels identically. The picture shows simple flowers created with chain stitch. Six-pointed stars (using stem stitch) would also be appropriate.

4. With wrong sides together, slip the lining 'cap' into the velvety/silky 'cap'.

5. Turn in curved edges and finish with cross stitch or herringbone stitch for decoration and firmness.

6. A button sewn in the centre on the top, where the points meet, will disguise the bulk and hide any mismatches!

CENTRE

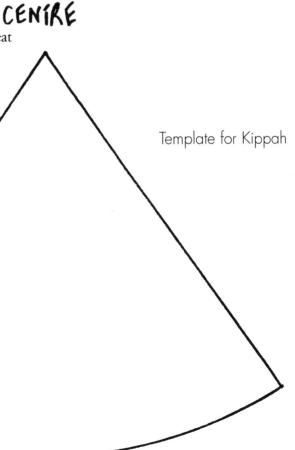

Template for Kippah

TIKEL

(head scarf)

What you need

- a plain white gent's handkerchief (this will make two)
- 50cm white lace or trimming, 1-3cm wide
- white thread

What you do

1. Cut the handkerchief in half diagonally.
2. Fold raw edge over about 0.5cm.
3. Cut lace to length of edge, allowing 1 cm at each end to turn in neatly.
4. Attach lace to edge so that it extends beyond it.

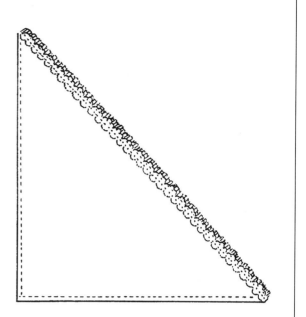

TALLIT BAG

(bag for prayer shawl)

What you need

- 50 x 30cm felt (or other non-fraying heavy fabric) in navy, royal, maroon or other dark colour. If velvet or other fraying fabric is used, the bag will need to be lined, using same size lining fabric and allowing 1-2 cm seams.
- 2 x 3cm strips of double-sided Velcro (optional)
- matching thread
- contrasting thread, preferably gold or silver

Note

The bag will measure 30cm wide and 20cm deep, with a flap 10cm deep.

What you do

1. Fold fabric over 20cm on the 50cm side. Stitch evenly, allowing a seam of 0.5cm on both sides of the flap.
2. The flap may be secured by attaching a strip of Velcro on each side at both ends.
3. Decorate the flap with flowers in daisy stitch or six-pointed stars in chain stitch.

TALLIT

(prayer shawl)

What you need

- 124 x 50cm cream (or white) fabric, such as polyester cotton
- matching thread
- 1m fringing in matching shade
- 45 x 10cm decorative fabric, such as broderie anglaise, in matching colour
- blue fabric paint or crayons
- 12m cream embroidery thread

What you do

1. Turn 0.5cm on all edges and turn again. Stitch neatly.

2. Attach fringing to both short ends.

3. To make neck piece, turn 0.5cm on all edges of decorative fabric and attach to the middle of one edge of the large piece of fabric on the right side, as shown.

4. Paint blue stripes, as shown.

5. To make tzitzit (knotted and bound threads), for each corner: cut from the cream embroidery thread 1 x 1m (for the shamash, 'servant' thread) and 3 x 60cm lengths. Trying not to break the threads of the fabric, make a hole about 4 cm each way from the corner of the tallit. Even up the 4 embroidery threads at one end and push or thread them through the hole. Bring the short threads together and allow the long thread (shamash) to hang freely. Holding 4 threads in each hand, tie a granny knot near the edge of the tallit.

   Separate the shamash and make 7 complete winds round the other threads. Follow with a second granny knot. Then wind the shamash 8 times round the others. Tie the third granny knot and wind the shamash 11 times round the others. Tie another granny knot and finally wind the shamash 13 times round the others. Finish with a granny knot and do not trim the ends of the threads.

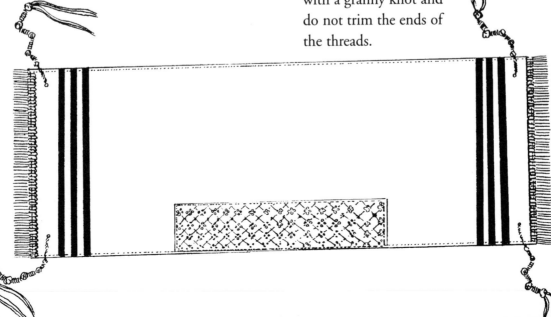

CUBE FRAMEWORK

What you need

- lengths of wooden batten all 12mm x 12mm: 12 pieces 1.5m in length and 2 pieces 2.15m in length

- 8 'Teko' corners (made by Osmiroid) or similar

- masking tape

- wood glue or 8 small tacks

- varnish (optional)

Note

- Some wood stores only sell batten by imperial measurement. If this is the case, buy slightly thinner batten and bind ends with masking tape to fit snugly into the corners.

- If 'Teko' is unavailable, other corners (such as those sold by office suppliers, for connecting screens) may be substituted: they must have slots or clips which can take a vertical pole and two horizontals at right-angles. A different width of batten may have to be used. If they do not have a slot or clip in a diagonal position, tie strings diagonally across the finished cube to support the draped cloth. Educational construction systems (such as 'Quadro') may be used and will make a very rigid frame: choose a neutral colour.

What you do

1. If using varnish, apply to edges of all pieces of batten and allow to dry thoroughly.

2. To make the uprights, fit two 'Teko' corners to each of the 4 shorter pieces of batten, ensuring that the diagonal point of each 'Teko' corner points in the same direction on each piece. Secure each corner with a small amount of glue or a tack through one of the holes in the 'Teko' corner.

3. The 8 remaining short lengths of batten will form the horizontal sides of the frame (top and bottom). They need to fit snugly into the 'Teko' corners yet be capable of being dismantled and stored when the cube is not in use. Bind both ends of each piece of batten with sufficient masking tape to ensure this optimum fit.

4. The 2 longer pieces of batten will form the diagonals which give the frame additional stability and prevent the cloth drape from sagging in the middle. Bind both ends of each piece with masking tape, as above.

'CUDDLY' TORAH

This is a modern, rather than traditional, educational toy for young Jewish children.

What you need

- template
- for body: 2 pieces felt 30 x 30cm each, preferably red or royal blue
- for felt pages of book: 1 piece felt 22 x 22cm, preferably yellow or orange, cut into 4 equal pieces
- for book cover: 1 piece felt in different colour
- white paper, cut into 8 x 11cm squares
- thread in matching or contrasting colour(s)
- kapok for stuffing
- 'jester' bells, if possible

What you do

1. Use the 8 sheets of paper to make 'paper' pages. Either use children's drawing and writing, based on listening to and discussing stories from the Torah, or write out a selection of brief paraphrases of extracts from the Torah or thoughts about the Torah, such as: 'Love me very much. See my crown and pretty bells. I am special.' – 'The tinkling bells sing, 'I am the Torah' – 'The lions guard me. Help to take care of me, too.' – 'God's words are in the Torah and they are very beautiful.' – 'I am your God and I love you. Love me, too.' – 'Treat new people kindly and make friends.' – 'You must tell the truth.'

2. Attach paper pages to the front and back of all the felt pages, either with adhesive or with running stitches.

3. Photocopy template and use to cut out two body pieces.

4. Assemble pages and cover to form book, opening from right to left.

5. Stitch book in place on a body piece – which will then be the front.

6. Either cut out shapes of symbols in felt and attach them to the front of the body or draw or paint directly onto body.

7. With the right side of the front facing outwards, join the front and the back of the body together with running stitches, leaving a gap for stuffing. Use backstitch or blanket stitch: it must look neat on both sides.

8. Stuff lightly to give slightly rounded and floppy feel.

9. Close gap.

10. Attach bells, if used, to the top of Torah.

HUPAH

(Wedding canopy)

A hupah is not necessarily blue but this one is very effective. It is designed to fit the cube framework – instructions for which follow.

What you need

- 4.8m pale blue satin lining fabric, 120cm wide; any light-weight pale fabric which is cheaper or more readily available may be substituted
- matching sewing thread
- masking tape
- 10m matching ribbon, 5cm wide
- 8m each of white, pale blue and dark blue ribbon, cut into 1m lengths

Note

- This canopy is designed to lay over the basic cube (see p.00).
- Florist's ribbon is cheap and easy to use but, as it cannot be ironed, fold canopy away carefully after use and keep in a box out of reach!

What you do

1. Cut fabric in half and join two halves together by a narrow seam, to form a square.

2. Turn edges of square approximately 0.5cm on to wrong side, turn again and stitch.

3. Attach ribbon trim on right side.

4. Place canopy over cube and straighten all round so that it falls evenly. Mark the corners of the cube on the canopy.

5. Take four pieces of the same colour of florist's ribbon and cut each one into thin strips lengthways, up to about 10cm from the end. To curl ribbon, roll strips over a pencil, hold in place with masking tape and steam over

boiling water. When dry, remove tape and pencil. Lightly stitch the uncurled end of each piece to the corner mark on the canopy, on the underside.

6. Create looser curls of ribbon, through the rolling and steaming process using a cotton reel or large kitchen roll tube.

7. Add curls of ribbon to the canopy corners on the top side. A combination of narrow and wide strips, tight and loose curls, in three colours, creates an attractive effect: it is important to work in fours of ribbon lengths so that all the corners will be decorated in the same way. Finish each corner with a bow or coil of ribbon to hide the ends!

8. When laying finished canopy over cube, hold it in place on the underside with a hinge of masking tape.

Hupah, with ribbon falls on cube

4. FOOD

HALLAH (Challah)

Hallah is a plaited loaf of enriched dough. Two hallot, covered by a cloth, are served at each of the three Sabbath meals in an observant Jewish home – on Friday evening, Saturday lunchtime and Saturday afternoon/evening. The three meals and the three strands in each loaf symbolise the relationship between God, Torah (teaching) and Israel (people) which is a theme of the day. In ancient days, the hallah was a piece of dough which the priest would throw into a fire as part of the sacrifices.

Note

Taking hallah: if three or more pounds of flour are made into dough for bread, 'hallah' has to be taken. A small portion of the dough (not less than the size of a large olive) is removed and the following blessing is recited: 'Blessed are you, Lord our God, ruler of the Universe who makes us holy with his commandments and has commanded us to set apart this bread.' The piece of dough is then burnt.

What you need

- 12g fresh yeast or 25g dried yeast
- 1 teaspoon sugar
- warm water
- 450g strong plain flour
- 1 teaspoon salt
- 2 tablespoons oil
- 1 egg
- beaten egg to glaze
- poppy seeds (optional)

What you do

Note

The unbaked hallah can be left in a refrigerator overnight in the polythene bag and then put in a warm place until doubled in size the next day, before baking.

1. Mix together the yeast, sugar and 2 tablespoons warm water and leave until bubbly. This will take 5-10 minutes.

2. Mix together the flour and salt.

3. Make a well in the centre of the flour and add one egg, yeast mixture and enough warm water, gradually, to make into a stiff dough. Beat very well.

4. Turn onto a board and knead for 5 minutes.

5. Divide into six.

6. Knead each piece and roll into a long strip.

7. Make into two loaves by plaiting three strands together.

8. Place on a greased and floured tin. Brush with water.

9. Slip into a greased polythene bag, and leave in a warm place until doubled in size.

10. Brush with the beaten egg and sprinkle with poppy seeds.

11. Bake in the oven at 400°F, Mark 6 for 10 minutes, then reduce the heat to 350°F, Mark 4 for 45 minutes.

'PEACEFUL' CHOLENT

Cholent is a luncheon dish on the Sabbath (Saturday). It is an extremely slow-cooking casserole which is designed to be a hot Sabbath meal that requires no work on the day itself. The recipe for cholent will vary from community to community, but has beans as its basis. Cholent usually contains meat, though only a little and 'cheap' cut that requires long slow cooking. But here is a foolproof vegetarian recipe. Ladle the cholent on to warm plates and serve with hallah.

What you need

- 110g dried beans (preferably a variety of shapes and sizes; they must be soaked for at least 12 hours in advance)
- 450g onions, peeled and finely sliced or chopped
- oil for frying
- 450g potatoes, cut into large chunks
- 25g pearl barley or buckwheat
- vegetables for flavour – about two of the following: a large carrot, small parsnip, piece of swede, stick of celery
- 1 bouquet garni
- 6 bay leaves
- 2 large cloves of garlic (crushed or chopped)
- 850ml of boiling water, flavoured with 1 dessertspoon yeast extract, a few squirts of soy sauce, a little dried paprika, a few pinches of chives and a vegetable stock cube
- raw eggs, in their shells – one per adult equivalent (optional)

Note

- Do not add salt at the cooking stage as it would make the bean skins tough: there is sufficient salt in the yeast extract and the stock cube.

- The cholent will need to be slow-cooked for 15 – 20 hours, so prepare and assemble ingredients sufficiently in advance.

What you do

1. Drain soaking water off beans.
2. Place them in a saucepan with fresh water, the bay leaves and bouquet garni.
3. Boil the beans vigorously, keeping them well covered with water for at least 20 minutes. This is especially important if your selection of beans includes red kidney beans: if not cooked sufficiently, they can cause violent illness!
4. Remove the bouquet garni (but not the bay leaves).
5. Meanwhile fry the onions and garlic gently until golden in colour.
6. Combine the onion, beans and uncooked pearl barley with the chopped raw vegetables and turn into a casserole dish which has a tightly fitting lid. (If the lid does not fit well, a large piece of foil can be pressed down firmly around the sides as far as the bottom of the dish.
7. Pour over the flavoured boiling water. Add more water, if necessary, to ensure that the mixture is well covered.
8. If you are using eggs, add about 6 – raw and unshelled but washed. Push them carefully into the mixture.
9. Cover the dish with the lid or foil.
10. Place the cholent in an oven, set to the lowest possible heat, or in an electric 'slow cooker'. Leave the heat on all the time.
11. When ready to serve, remove the eggs (if you have included them) with a spoon to avoid scalding the fingers, run them under a cold tap, and shell them. They will have the consistency of hard-boiled eggs, but the 'whites' will be brown. They will have absorbed the flavour of the cholent and can be served as an appetiser – alone or with pickles.

HAROSET (CHAROSET)

Haroset is a sweet and sticky paste. It is one of the elements of the ceremonial Seder meal at Passover, and represents the mortar used by the Hebrew slaves in Egypt. It is also linked with the overall theme of the meal which is the mixing of bitter with sweet and, like the other symbolic foods, it recalls both the slavery and the freedom commemorated at this time. Textures and tastes vary from community to community – and from family to family – but haroset is mostly based on apples or dates, nuts, and wine or grape juice.

Note
The haroset should turn reddish brown as you make it.

What you need
- 3 apples
- 1 teaspoon of cinnamon
- half cup of nuts – chopped or ground or a mixture of both
- 2 tablespoons sweet, red grape juice
- a little honey, if liked

What you do
1. Peel the apples, remove the cores and grate into a bowl.
2. Add the other ingredients and mix thoroughly.

5. BOOKS
SIMPLIFIED TEXTS OF TRADITIONAL PRAYERS

EVENING PRAYERS FOR CHILDREN

Everlasting God, help me to sleep peacefully and be good in the daytime. Help me to be peaceful and protect me because you are good.

God who looks over people doesn't sleep or have a nap. God will take care of you as you come and go, now and for ever.

Listen people, our God, the Everlasting God, is one. You will love God with your whole heart, with your whole self and with your whole strength.

I let God look after my soul and my body all day and all night. God is close to me and I feel safe.

Blessed be God by day. Blessed be God by night. Blessed be God when we go to sleep. Blessed be God when we get up.

May God's helpers take care of me. May they protect me. May they give me strength. May they give me light. May they keep me safe. May God always be in my life.

MORNING PRAYERS FOR CHILDREN

You are blessed, Everlasting God, carer of the world, who helps us to wake up from our sleep.

Everlasting God, you are my carer. You give me all I need. You let me be in lovely places. I will always have goodness and kindness while you are caring for me. I will live with you for ever.

Help me to think of God while I am alone and when I am with others. Help me to tell the truth and have the truth in my heart.

God, please help me not to say nasty things about others or to tell lies. Help me to love the words you say and have them in my heart. Help me to do as you want.

God, help everything I say and everything in my heart to be what you want. You give me strength.

The wolf shall live with the lamb. The leopard lie down with the kid. The calf and the young lion shall feed together, and a little child shall lead them. They shall not hurt or destroy in all your holy mountain.

SIMPLIFIED, PARAPHRASED EXTRACTS FROM TEXT OF HAGGADAH, BOOK FOR SEDER (PASSOVER SUPPER)

We light the candles to start the meal.

You are wonderful, Everlasting God. You make the grapes for juice and wine.

Everlasting God, thank you for taking care of us. We have our first drink of grape juice.

You are wonderful, Everlasting God. You made all the food in the earth. We dip a green vegetable in salty water. It tastes like the tears the slaves cried when they were sad.

Now it is time to hide the matzah. People ate flat bread when they were slaves and were sad. Anyone who is hungry can eat with us now. Let us all be free next year.

How is tonight different from other nights?

We eat only matzah for our bread.

We eat only bitter vegetables for our vegetables.

We dip our vegetables twice.

We all lean at table.

God got us out of a horrid place where we were picked on and bullied. God wants everyone to be free.

Ten horrid things happened to try and make the horrid people let us go free. We spill a bit of grape juice when we say each of the ten horrid things. It shows that we are sorry that people got hurt – even if they were horrid – when we were let free. Blood... frogs... nits... creepy crawlies... sores... boils... locusts... hail... darkness... babies dying

These foods remind us of important things:

Bitter vegetables

Bitter vegetables taste horrid. The people were horrid to us when they picked on us and bullied us.

Lamb's bone

Lambs make us think of being free.

Matzah

Matzah is flat. When we left the horrid place, we took our bread in a hurry and it stayed flat.

We try to feel sad like the people did in the place where we were picked on and bullied. It helps us to feel like people today who are unhappy and not free. But we feel happy that God makes us free. Thank you, God.

You made the grapes. You are wonderful, Everlasting God. We have our second drink.

We wash our hands. You are wonderful, Everlasting God. You made all the food in the earth. You are wonderful, Everlasting God.

Someone breaks the matzah and we all share it.

You are wonderful, Everlasting God.

We eat a piece of bitter vegetable with haroset. Haroset is a bit like cement. We eat it because the people in the horrid place had to do lots of building work and they had hardly any food or sleep.

Now we make a matzah sandwich with a bitter vegetable.

We have our meal now.

We hunt for the hidden matzah. Whoever finds it gets a prize.

We share the matzah. You are wonderful, Everlasting God. You make enough food for everyone. We must share it because you want us to.

You are wonderful, Everlasting God. You made the grapes. We have our third drink.

1.

2. 16. 27. 29.

1. 16. 27. 29

3. 18.

4.

6. 12.

5.

6.

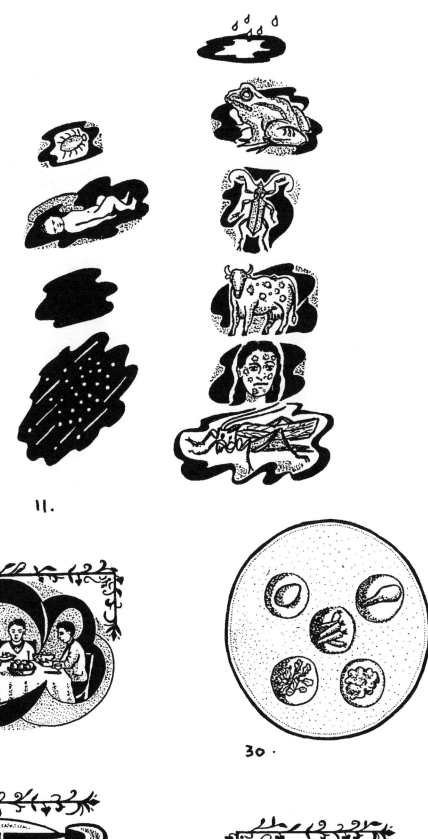

11.

28.

30.

28.

30.

17.

21.

19.

20.

22.

24.

23.

25.

7.

8.

7.

9.

10.

14.

13.

15.

Chapter 6 **BEING IN A MUSLIM HOME**

Most of the Muslims who were interviewed by the 'Home Team' characterised their family life as a fusion of religious discipline and mutual fulfilment. Most Muslim homes contain a copy of the Qur'an and, although it is not always immediately visible, it occupies a place of importance – on the highest shelf – and is kept covered when not in use. As revealed scripture, the Qur'an plays a significant role in the shaping of religious sensibility and ethical principles. Muslim children are encouraged to memorise the Qur'an in Arabic, whatever language they speak, and many have committed it all to memory. They often refer to the Qur'an and – of secondary importance- to the Hadith (sayings of The Prophet) or the Sirah (biography of The Prophet) when taking decisions or explaining a principle.

One of the many ways in which discipline is expressed is in observance of the five times of daily prayer (dawn, noon, afternoon, evening and night). Prayer can be offered on any clean place, not only in a mosque, and families usually pray together when they are at home at these times. Either males and females pray in separate rooms or the women and girls stand behind the men and boys. Wudhu (washing before prayer) takes place under running water, usually in the bathroom.

Other exercise of discipline relates to food. Halal (permitted) food is: the meat of sheep, goats, cows and poultry which has been slaughtered by a butcher who says, "In the name of Allah, Allah is most Great"; edible plants; eggs of halal birds; milk from halal mammals; and edible fish. Haram (forbidden) food and drink is: meat and meat products from pigs; the meat of any animal which has died naturally or has been strangled; carnivorous animals; alcohol. Within these boundaries, Muslims may eat any kinds of dishes. During the month of Ramadan, adult Muslims fast completely during the hours of daylight, unless they are prevented by their physical condition.

Dress, too, reflects Islamic principles. Both males and females are required to dress modestly but dress that is suitable for Muslim men and boys is seldom distinctive of male attire worn by men of other groups and today many Muslims wear western dress. The Qur'an spells out in detail what modest dress means for women when they are with men who are not close relatives: all but their hands, feet and faces should be covered and garments should be loose and opaque. But the general rule of modesty applies to men and to women. Muslim men and women can dress in a style that suits the climate where they live and is in keeping with its culture, provided that it is modest.

Muslims are encouraged to marry and enjoy family life, and the Qur'an says more about this than any other topic. A Muslim man may have up to four wives if he can provide and care for them all equally but most have only one wife. A Muslim woman may only have one husband. A Muslim man may marry a Muslim, Christian or

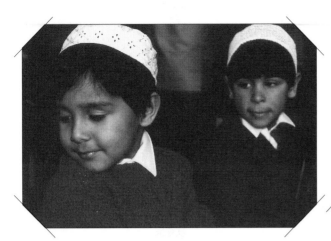

Jewish woman. A Muslim woman should marry a Muslim man. Muslims see babies as blessings, as gifts from Allah.

The wife does not have to use the money and property that she had when she married to support herself or her children: this is her husband's responsibility. Her main responsibility is to provide an Islamic home for her family. She may take a job and follow her career as long as it does not interfere with this.

For Muslims, Islam dates from the creation of the world but it emerged as a distinct religious system in Arabia about 1500 years ago. Through missionary journeys and the conquest of surrounding lands, Islam spread rapidly in the first few centuries and is again gaining new converts in the 20th century. It is the fastest growing religion today and it is estimated that about one-sixth of the world's population is Muslim. Muslim individuals and communities and political events in Islamic countries are often in the news and media coverage may be a useful topical resource for older pupils but they should be alerted to the anti-Islamic bias which much of it contains.

Islam is unequivocally monotheistic (believing in only one God) and shares many characteristics with Judaism and Christianity. Muslims believe that Adam was the first Prophet of Islam and he was followed by other Jewish leaders and teachers, including Musa (Moses), Dawud (David) and Isa (Jesus). However, people drifted away from the truth taught by the Prophets and Allah sent a final messenger, the Prophet Muhammad, whom Muslims refer to as the 'Seal of the Prophets'. When naming a Prophet, Muslims say 'Peace be upon Him' and, when writing a Prophet's name, they follow it in English with the abbreviation 'pbuh'.

Because Allah (God) is pure spirit, with no partner, no parents and no offspring, Muslims do not compare Allah to human beings through metaphors and similes but rather use adjectives to express Allah's qualities, for example,

'Merciful'. Likewise, they do not depict Allah in figurative art. Islamic art and architecture nevertheless expresses religious ideas and values, mainly through the use of calligraphy of verses from the Qur'an, geometric patterns and a distinctive design known as 'arabesque' – a repeating swirling pattern that evokes flowers and foliage. With a few notable exceptions (for example in some Persian schools of art), Islamic art also avoids depicting Prophets and Caliphs (leaders who succeeded the Prophet Muhammad).

When teaching about Islam, it is therefore sensitive to avoid asking any pupils to depict their concept of Allah or to draw pictures of events involving the Prophets or Caliphs; and, equally, to avoid dramatisation or role plays of these events. While photography and figurative art of secular subjects are permissible in Islam, some Muslim pupils may have been taught to avoid it altogether and may be reluctant to engage in it at school: when offering pupils artistic activities, it is therefore helpful to provide an equally attractive and valuable alternative.

The terms 'Muslim' and 'Islamic' sometimes cause confusion. The adherents of Islam are called 'Muslims' and the term derives from the same Arabic root as 'Islam' (roughly equivalent to 'SLM') which means 'submission' or 'peace'. 'Islamic' is used to refer to aspects of religion and culture so that you might say, for example, 'an Islamic country' or 'Islamic art'. Generally, Muslims are keen to make a distinction between that which is essential to Islamic teaching – and therefore revealed truth – and that which happens to be a cultural manifestation of Islam in a given society. The single most populous ethnic group of Muslims in Britain originates from the Indian sub-continent, notably Bangladesh and Pakistan. Cultural examples (such as food and dress) in *Homing In* are drawn from the culture of such families living in Britain.

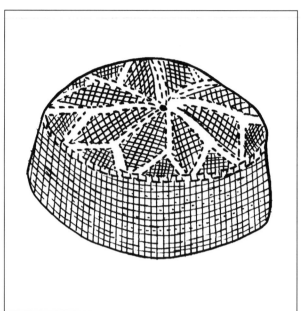

2.'DOORWAYS' TO A MUSLIM HOME

WATER
specific to Islam

English
- ❏ use of Qur'an and its language
- ❏ Arabic/English script
- ❏ multilingual stories and poems
- ❏ composing prayers
- ❏ writing invitations to home corner occasions
- ❏ reading and writing water poems and stories

Mathematics
- ❏ shape and sequencing games
- ❏ rotation and tessellation
- ❏ geometric patterns
- ❏ symmetry
- ❏ counting patterns
- ❏ number 99 (tazbi) made up of 3 x 33 – example of factors
- ❏ number 5 (prayers a day, pillars) – examples in everyday life

Science
- ❏ properties of water
- ❏ functions of water – life-giving, cleansing, refreshing

Technology
- ❏ making a Qur'an
- ❏ making a Qur'an stand
- ❏ making sajjadah (prayer mat)
- ❏ making instruments for watery sounds

History
- ❏ biography of The Prophet

Geography
- ❏ plan of a mosque
- ❏ mosques in relation to school e.g. distance to the nearest mosque

Art
- ❏ colour mixing with water and painting with water colours
- ❏ making Islamic tiles by painting and weaving
- ❏ creating Islamic patterns

Music
- ❏ making watery music
- ❏ listening to music on water theme e.g. Handel's 'Water Music'

Physical education
- ❏ simulating wudhu (washing before prayer in the Islamic tradition)

Religious education
- ❏ cleanliness before reading Qur'an
- ❏ preparation for prayer through wudhu
- ❏ use of sajjadah (prayer mat)
- ❏ call to prayer
- ❏ praying five times a day
- ❏ form and function of the mosque
- ❏ visiting a mosque

BUILDINGS
generic but with emphasis on Islam

English
- building vocabulary, including appropriate technical terms
- listening to prayers from various religious traditions
- examining various scripts
- composing prayers
- creating journey stories
- poems about special times and journeys
- writing instructions for mosque model
- letters to request visit to a mosque or in thanks for one

Mathematics
- the number 5 (praying five times a day, the 'Five Pillars')
- symmetry
- tessellation of shape and pattern
- measurements and coordinates

Science
- need for foundations
- building materials and their properties
- water-proofing and insulation
- size of windows

Technology
- designing and making a model of a mosque, with minaret, qibla wall and mihrab, wudhu (washing) area...

History
- history of a particular mosque

Geography
- location of mosques in locality/Britain
- the town of Makkah
- planning a hajj
- the qibla (direction of Makkah)
- compass directions
- using a Makkah compass

Art
- decorating maps
- decorating a model mosque
- observational drawing of buildings
- printing patterns
- the features of Islamic art

Music
- rhythm of prayer
- spoken/sung prayers

Physical education
- simulating sequence of prayer movements
- prayer (not Islamic) through dance

Religious education
- visiting a mosque
- concepts of a special place
- experience of awe and wonder in buildings
- the functions of places of worship and religious community buildings

3.'FURNISHINGS'

QUR'AN STAND

What you need

- templates for two sections of stand
- thick cardboard, approximately A2 size
- 3m balsa wood, 1.25 x 0.5 cm thick
- balsa wood cement
- sharp craft knife
- cutting mat or board
- hack saw
- sandpaper
- brown wood stain or renovating shoe polish
- PVA

Note

The stand is assembled by slotting the two sections together; it can be stored flat.

What you do

1. Photocopy one of the templates and use it to cut two pieces of cardboard with craft knife.

2. Using the hack saw, cut strips of balsa wood to fit round all edges.

3. Stick wide sides of balsa wood strips flush to the edges of cardboard.

4. Spread more cement on balsa wood strips and lay matching piece of cardboard on top, ensuring that it fits exactly all the way round.

5. Weight or peg, and leave to dry thoroughly.

6. Repeat steps 1-5 for the other section of the stand.

7. Sand all rough edges.

8. Stain, or apply shoe polish, to all surfaces. Leave to dry thoroughly.

9. 'Varnish' both sides of each section with PVA.

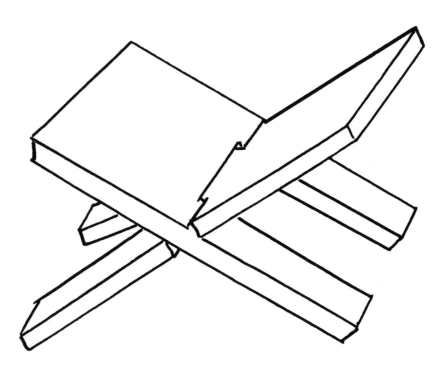

Process of making Qur'an Stand

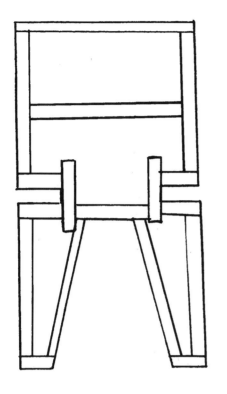

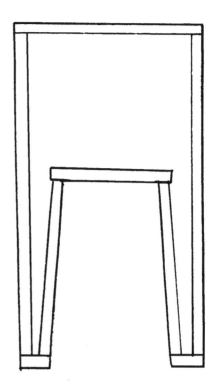

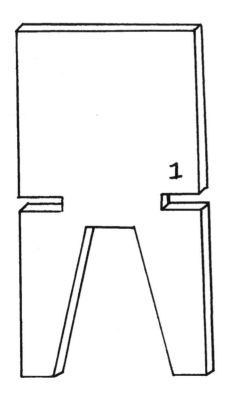

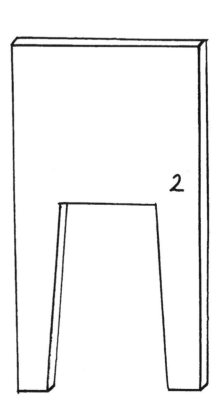

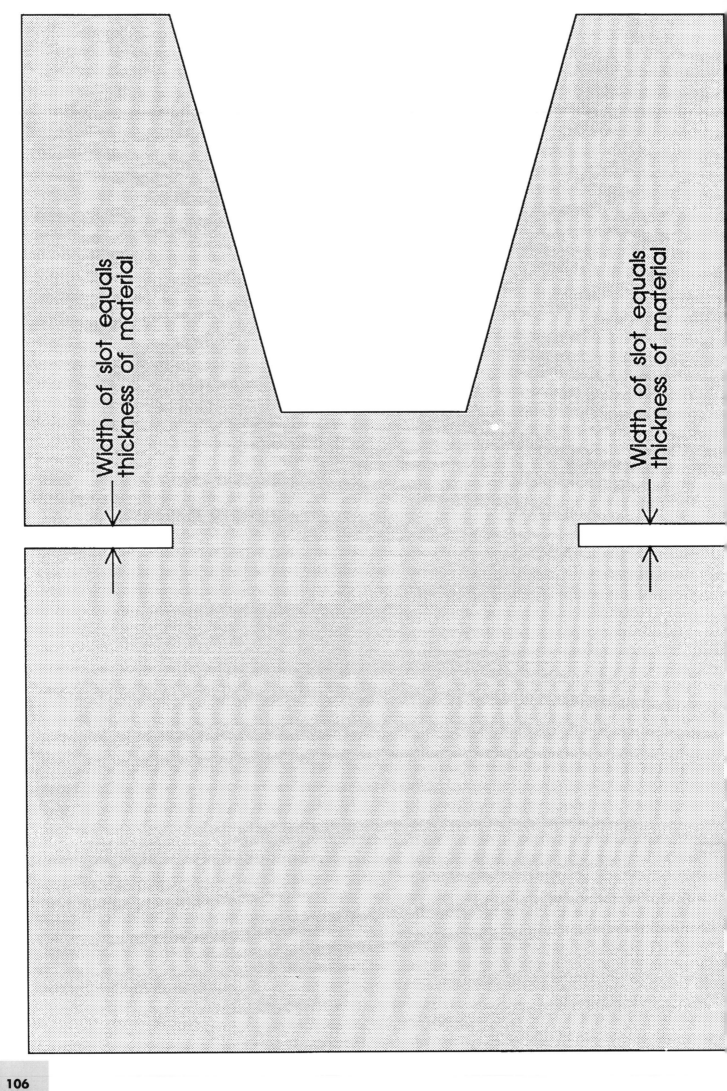

Width of slot equals
thickness of material

Width of slot equals
thickness of material

QUR'AN COVER

What you need

- 50cm x 25 cm silky or shiny fabric, green or neutral in colour, plain or with slight self-pattern

- 50cm x 25cm heavy fabric, such as brocade, in complementary colour, also plain or with slight self-pattern

- 150cm soft fringing in complementary colour – silver or gold would give appropriate effect

- 1m cord in complementary colour

- matching thread

- 150cm ribbon trim in complementary colour (optional)

What you do

1. Place the right sides of the two pieces of fabric together.

2. Stitch along both long sides and one short side, about 0.5 cm from edge.

3. Mitre corners, turn inside out and press.

4. Turn in edges on remaining short side and stitch.

5. If using ribbon trim, attach it to all edges of heavy fabric, turning in ends of ribbon neatly.

6. On shiny/silky fabric, attach soft fringing on all sides so that fringing extends beyond the edge; turn in ends of fringing neatly.

7. Attach centre of cord to centre of a short side.

8. Cover the Qur'an by placing it on the heavy fabric side and folding the cloth round the book so that the silky/shiny fabric is then on the outside. Wind cord round the Qur'an and tie with a bow.

Qur'an with cover, on stand

PRAYER CAP

What you need

- piece of mock broderie anglaise, thick lace curtaining or other open-weave fabric in white or cream: if buying new fabric, a 25cm x 1m length is ample

- matching thread.

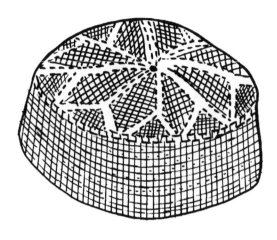

What to do

1. Cut a circle of fabric 16cm in diameter. Cut a strip of fabric 53cm x 7cm: if necessary, join together 7cm strips to achieve same length.

2. Form a circular band by joining together the two ends of the strip, with the right sides facing; allow 0.5cm for seam.

3. With right sides facing, ease the circular band on to the edge of the circle of fabric. Allowing 0.5cm for seam, stitch very securely.

4. Turn over lower edge and stitch neatly.

TAZBI

(prayer beads)

What you need

- 33 identical small round plain beads, preferably green or neutral in colour, of any material

- strong thread

- embroidery thread (same colour as beads if possible).

What you do

1. String beads onto thread, leave a small gap (about 0.5cm). Tie very firmly.

2. Cut about 20 pieces of embroidery silk, each about 10cm long.

3. Hold lengths together and double over. Place under gap in beads.

4. Pass ends of embroidery silk through the loop and pull tightly to create tassel.

PRAYER MAT

What you need

- piece approximately 50cm x 70cm chromo-moss material (such as 'Vivelle' by Dryad) or other textured fabric with paper backing, preferably green

- other pieces of same material in colours according to preferred design

- 1m soft fringing in appropriate colour

- PVA

Note

When designing prayer mat, avoid human or animal figures and the crucifix form. A design based on a mosque or an Islamic site is complicated but authentic and satisfying to create. Otherwise aim for a symmetrical abstract design.

What you do

1. On the back of the various pieces of chromo-moss (or other textured material), draw shapes using the templates given or mathematics/technology pieces.

2. Cut out small pieces and arrange on large piece.

3. Stick small pieces on to large piece, apply weights and leave to dry.

4. Cut fringing in two.

5. Turn in ends of each piece of fringing and attach one piece to each short end of the mat.

MUSLIM WALL PLAQUE – NAME OF ALLAH

What you need

- 'name' in calligraphy
- sequins or pieces of shiny paper
- gold/silver crayons
- short piece of cord, ribbon or string for hanging
- paper plate or circle of card
- PVA

What you do

1. Photocopy 'name', cut out carefully and stick on to plate or card.
2. Colour 'name' in gold or silver.
3. Decorate plaque with sequins or shiny paper.
4. Make loop and attach for hanging.

MUSLIM WALL PLAQUE – PICTURE OF SITE

What you need

- either picture (such as on postcard) of Makkah, Madinah or other Islamic site or photocopy of picture of site in this book (which can be reduced on photocopier)
- photocopy of 'framing' template
- thin card
- gold or silver crayons
- short piece of cord, ribbon or string for hanging
- PVA

What you do

1. Cut card slightly larger than picture.

2. Stick picture on to card.

3. Choose 'framing' and stick lengths all round picture, mitring the corners. Colour.

4. Attach a loop of string or cord on back for hanging.

The London Cenral Mosque in Regent's Park

The Prophet's Mosque in Madinah

The Dome of the Rock in Jerusalem

The Ka'aba in Makkah

Plaques on wall and mantelpiece

SHOE RACK

What you need

- 12 adult shoe boxes, all same size with lids, preferably in white or pale colours

- sugar paper or fairly plain wallpaper for covering

- strong stapler

- PVA

What you do

1. Cut one third off length of each box and lid, and discard.

2. Stick and/or staple lids to boxes, leaving one end open.

3. Stack boxes three wide and four high; stick and press firmly.

4. Cover all but open side with paper, to hide joins.

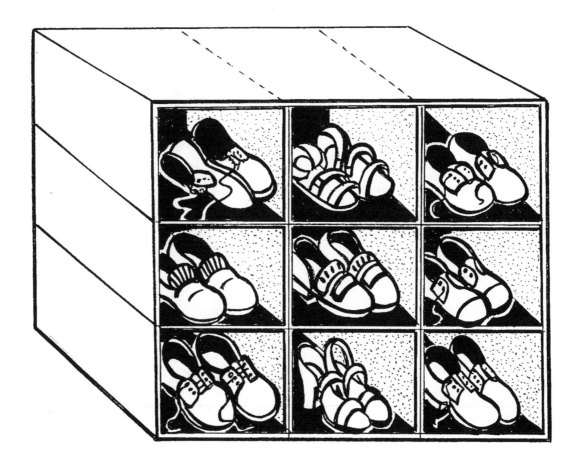

KURTA

(male suit)

See page 145

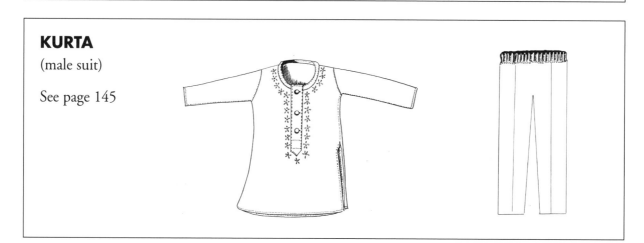

SHALWAR, KAMEEZ AND CHUNI

(girl's trousers, tunic and long scarf)

This is not a complicated outfit to make but does require some previous experience of dressmaking.

What you need

- for shalwar (trousers): 1m plain cotton, polyester or silk-like fabric, 1m wide
- for kameez (tunic): 70cm patterned cotton, polyester silk-like fabric, 1m wide in complementary colours
- for chuni (scarf): 1.5m x 50cm chiffon or other fine fabric in matching or complementary colours
- sewing thread
- 50cm narrow elastic

What you do

1. Make chuni by neatening all raw edges.

2. Use patterns provided to cut pieces of fabric for shalwar and kameez. Refer to picture detail when making up garments. When sewing up, allow a 1cm seam and neaten edges.

3. Face neck of kameez with strips cut from remaining fabric or, if insufficient, with bias binding.

4. On wrong side of shalwar, turn top over 1cm and turn over again. Machine firmly, leaving a small opening to pass elastic. Thread elastic through, adjusting to size required. Secure elastic with strong stitches.

Kameez

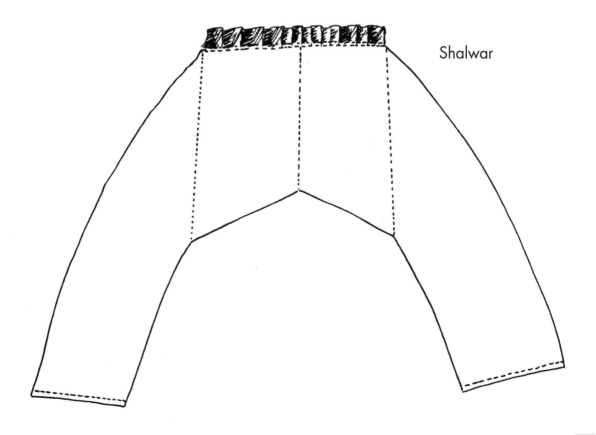

Shalwar

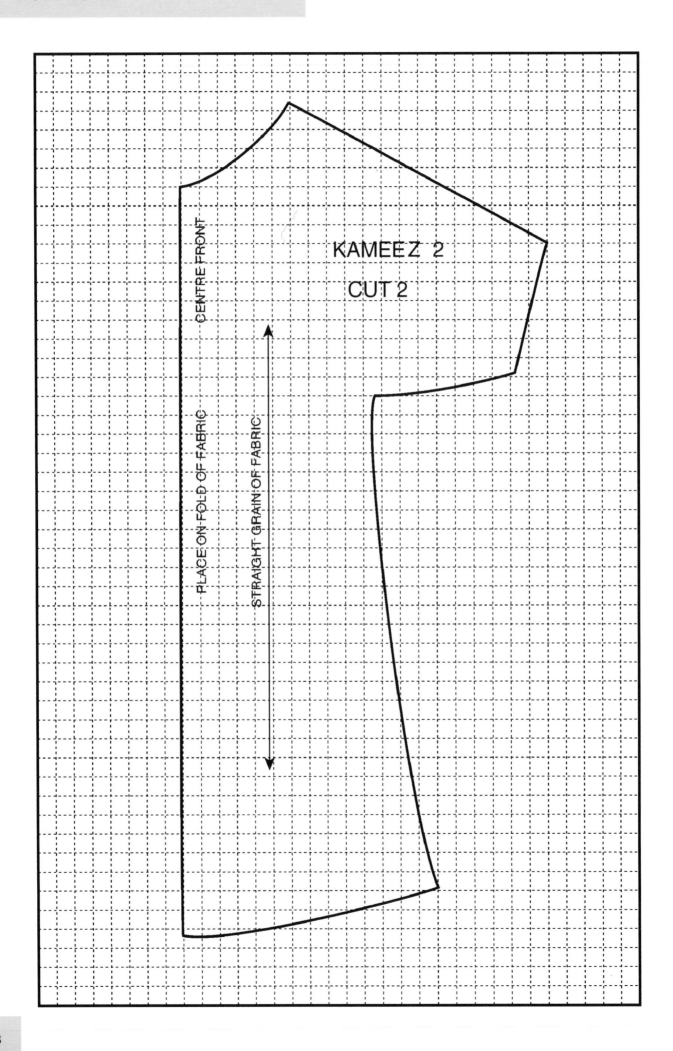

CENTRE FRONT

KAMEEZ 2

CUT 2

PLACE ON FOLD OF FABRIC

STRAIGHT GRAIN OF FABRIC

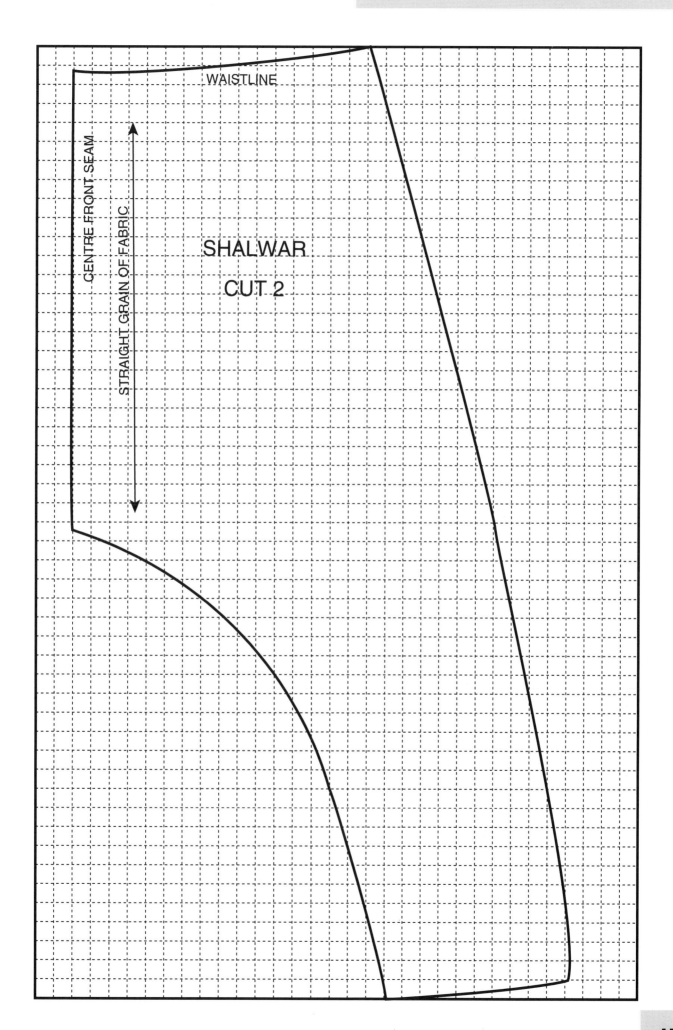

WAISTLINE

CENTRE FRONT SEAM.

STRAIGHT GRAIN OF FABRIC

SHALWAR

CUT 2

WAISTLINE

4. FOOD

PURIS

Traditionally puris are cooked in a deep cast-iron pan but a deep fryer may be used.

What you need
- 110g wholemeal flour
- 110g plain flour
- half teaspoon salt
- 25g butter (melted)
- oil for deep frying

What you do
1. Combine the dry ingredients in a large mixing bowl.
2. Make a hollow in the centre and pour in the melted butter.
3. Add the water gradually, kneading the mixture, until a firm dough is formed.
4. Cover with a damp cloth and set aside for 15 minutes.
5. Divide the dough into 8 pieces and roll each into a thick circle.
6. Fry the puris one at a time in the hot oil. After a few seconds the puri will puff up. When it is crisp and golden remove from the oil and drain on kitchen paper.

Note
Only adults should fry the puris.

KHEER

This is a rice-based sweet dish, which is ideal as a dessert. It can be served either hot or cold.

What you need
- 50g short grain rice
- 850ml milk
- 1 level tablespoon sugar
- 25g sultanas
- 25g blanched and chopped almonds
- 6 cardamom pods, finely crushed

What you do
1. Wash the rice thoroughly and put in a pan.
2. Pour over the milk, and stir thoroughly.
3. Cook on a medium heat for 30 – 45 minutes until the rice is soft and creamy.
4. Add the sugar and the other ingredients, mix well and leave to simmer for 5 minutes.
5. Serve hot, or allow to cool thoroughly and serve cold.

VEGETABLE CURRY

This is a delicious and simple recipe for a vegetable casserole. In the Indian sub-continent it would be ideal as a meal to break fast during the month of Ramadan, when Muslims cannot eat while the sun is up. All Muslims should observe this custom except for those who are sick, infirm or pregnant, for example. Young children are also exempt from the fast.

What you need

- 1 small cauliflower
- 175g carrots peeled and diced
- 225g broad beans
- 175g potatoes, peeled and diced
- 1 large onion, peeled and sliced
- 35g butter
- 1 tablespoon plain flour
- vegetable stock cube
- 2 tablespoons mango chutney
- black pepper
- 1 teaspoon ground cumin seed
- 1 teaspoon ground coriander
- 1 teaspoon chilli powder or finely chopped fresh chillies
- 1 teaspoon ginger
- salt
- 25g creamed coconut
- 150ml single cream

What you do

1. Steam the cauliflower, carrots and potatoes over boiling salted water for 10 minutes.

2. Cook the broad beans in boiling salted water for 5 minutes.

3. Drain the vegetables and keep warm. Reserve the cooking liquid from the broad beans.

4. Fry the onion in butter for 5 minutes over a low heat and increase heat to moderate. Fry, stirring, for 1 minute and stir in flour and spices and cook for a further minute; add chutney.

5. Measure 570ml of vegetable stock (made with broad bean cooking liquid) and pour onto curry mixture.

6. Stir in the vegetables, allowing them to heat through before serving.

5. BOOKS

(simplified, paraphrased extracts from the Qur'an)

People who are kind will have kindness and a lot more. They will not be ashamed and they will live happily for ever.

Tell people to go on a special journey and walk around our ancient building.

Ask Allah for help and wait. The world belongs to Allah.

Allah will be pleased with those who keep their promises and say their prayers.

When you pray, do not shout and do not whisper. Make your voice in between.

Do not say nasty things behind people's backs. How would you like it if someone did that to you?

Do not listen to people who say nasty things.

Praise to Allah, Lord of the world, who forgives us. We pray to you and want you to help us. Make us the way you want us to be.

Be close to each other. You are joined together by Allah. Do not split up. Allah loved you even when you were enemies. He brought you together like a family.

Never go into someone's house unless you know they want you to. Greet them politely. Allah knows whatever you do.

You will have peace because you have waited. In the end you will be very happy.

Do things together which make people happy. Do not do things together if they hurt people.

It is good to give things to people who need them.

If something bad happens to you, still be happy and good.

When people fall out, help them make friends again.

If you borrow something, make sure you give it back.

If you are asked to make room for someone, make room. Allah makes room for you.

You are really kind if you give someone something you really like.

When you are fasting, you can eat and drink until the white streak of dawn shows up against the black thread of night.

You cannot say, 'I will do that tomorrow'. You have to say, 'I will do that tomorrow if Allah lets me'.

Oh Allah is wonderful! Only Allah is God, the very special one. Allah made Heaven and Earth. Allah wraps the night up in the day and the day up in the night.

Border designs for Qur'an

Border designs for Qur'an

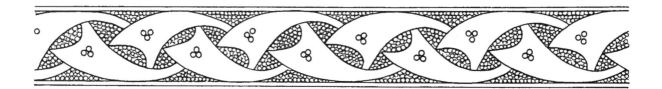

Chapter 7 **BEING IN A SIKH HOME**

From its beginning, Sikhism has valued family life and taught that it is not necessary to withdraw from the world to spiritual fulfilment: on the contrary, a verse in the Guru Granth Sahib (p. 661) says that people can find God through being in a family. The ten Gurus, who are guides and models for Sikhs, were all married – with the exception of the one who died at a very early age.

As with many communities in the Indian sub-continent or originating from the region, close-knit extended families are the norm: a couple lives together with not only their own children but also with their parents and maybe their grandparents, and their siblings and their grown-up families; sometimes the extended family is not housed under one roof but simply lives in very close proximity. This social system provides for a high degree of mutual responsibility and support and enables family members to fulfil the Sikh teachings that all generations and branches of a family should understand, respect and care for each other.

In Britain, the size of accommodation, the prevailing patterns of life in a modern secular society and the possible fragmentation of the family through migration and settlement create difficulties in maintaining family-wide daily contact and in sustaining the extended family. Nevertheless, many members of Sikh families try, whenever possible, to live close to each other.

In a Sikh marriage, men and women are equal partners and the Gurus emphasised the spiritual – as well as the social, emotional, intellectual and financial union – of husband and wife. The Gurus also taught that children are a gift from God, on trust to their parents. The concept and practice of service to others features large in a Sikh child's upbringing. A baby's name is chosen through opening the Guru Granth Sahib at random and choosing a name which begins with the initial of the first word at the top left hand corner of the open spread.

Worship is central to daily life in a Sikh home and begins in the morning, after washing or bathing. The day begins with Nam Japna – meditation on God's name, using scriptural passages – in any position or, if there is pressure of time, while dressing and getting things ready for the day. Children too young to be able to memorise scriptural passages at this time are encourage to recite 'Waheguru' (Wonderful Lord). At the evening and at bedtime, there are also special passages for recitation and meditation. Sikh worship has very little ritual, can be led by anyone and can take place anywhere.

If they can, Sikh families set aside a room or area of their home as a family gurdwara and where they keep a copy of the Guru Granth Sahib. At times there may be a Hukam, a random reading from the Guru Granth Sahib and Kirtan, devotional singing of compositions

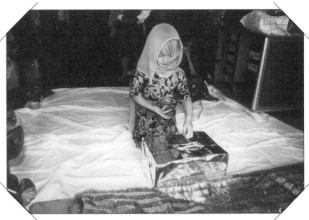

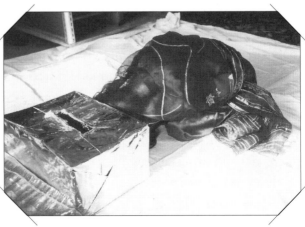

from the Guru Granth Sahib and other works. On special occasions, the family may arrange an Akhand Path and invite friends and members of the community to come for all or part of it: this is an unbroken reading of the entire Guru Granth Sahib by a chain of readers; it lasts about two days and nights.

Sikhism began in the 16th century in the Punjab, India, and was founded by Guru Nanak who grew up in a Hindu family. He questioned traditional Hindu teachings and practices concerning castes and stressed the equality of all people. The third guru, Guru Amar Das, encouraged everyone to eat together in the langar (the 'communal dining room' or 'free kitchen').

The fifth guru, Guru Arjan Dev, collected the writings of the first four gurus, his own writings and many Hindu and Islamic writings. This compilation was called the 'Adi Granth' and is now more commonly known as the Guru Granth Sahib. The tenth guru, Guru Gobind Singh, said that after him there would be no more human gurus and the Guru Granth Sahib would be the authority and guide for Sikhs. While all the gurus grew up in a society that was predominantly Hindu or Muslim and the Guru Granth Sahib reflects these traditions, Sikhs do not see their religion as a 'mixture' of Islam and Hinduism but as a revealed faith.

While there are Sikh missionaries and converts to Sikhism, Sikhism teaches the equality of all people and the value of all religions which they see as different paths to God. Sikhs believe that God has no form and no image, is never born and never dies, and is present everywhere. Guru Nanak said, 'There is neither Hindu nor Muslim, only God's path.' The fifth guru, Guru Arjan Dev, was tortured to death for refusing to convert to Islam or to alter the Guru Granth Sahib.

There are no 'sacred places' in Sikhism but the 'Harmandir Sahib' in Amritsar (often called the 'Golden Temple' by non-Sikhs) was built by Guru Arjan Dev and is the most important Sikh centre although it is not a formal pilgrimage site. Religious and political opposition to Sikhism has often centred on the Harmandir Sahib and it was attacked by opponents in 1984. This and the following events strengthened some Sikhs' resolve to achieve equality and recognition in Indian society today and to strive for Sikh autonomy in the Punjab.

Towards the end of the 19th century, Sikh men who were serving in the British army were posted overseas and many of them settled where they were stationed; civilian Sikh men also migrated, mainly to work and send money home; and British rulers in East Africa recruited Sikhs to build railways. Sikhs from the Punjab really began to settle in Britain in the 1950s. In the 1960s and 1970s many Sikhs left East Africa for Britain as the newly independent African countries became 'Africanised' and Asians were no longer welcome there. Sikhs had British passports and they or their families had given service to the British.

Today, about two-thirds of the Sikhs in Britain were born in Britain. The adults, especially the elderly, keep close ties with the Punjab but many younger Sikhs have never been there and think of themselves as British Sikhs. This affects the way they live, especially what they eat, how they dress and the language they speak. For example, a few do not speak Panjabi and many learn to read and write Panjabi at gurdwara schools. Sikhism is now practised all over the world, especially in English speaking countries, but the Punjab is still 'home'.

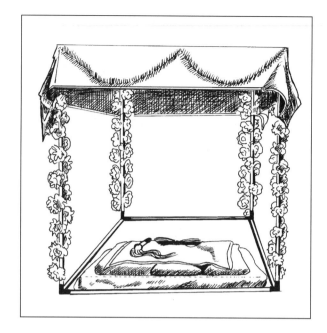

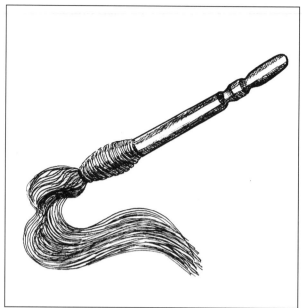

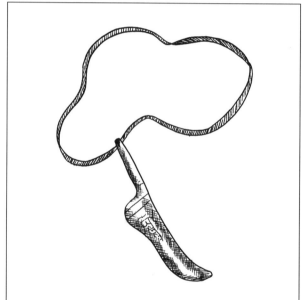

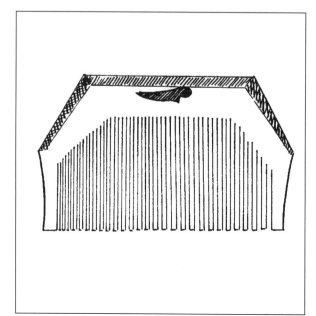

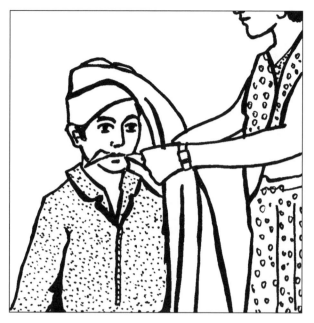

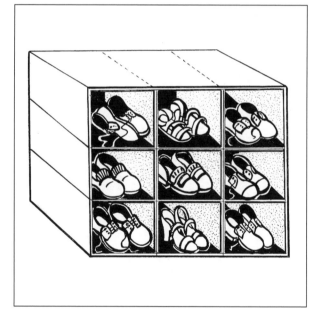

2. 'DOORWAYS' TO A SIKH HOME

HAIR
specific to Sikhism

English
- ❏ vocabulary for describing hair lengths, colours, textures, sheen and styles and for hair accessories (e.g. wig, clip)
- ❏ reading and writing stories poems and rhymes about hair and head coverings
- ❏ discussion about style and length of hair
- ❏ hair in the media – discussion of images in television and other commercials

Mathematics
- ❏ measuring hair length and hair growth over a period
- ❏ creating graphs of hair length and hair growth
- ❏ sorting beads and hair accessories
- ❏ matching games using pictures from magazines or photo sets

Science
- ❏ feely box (wigs, clips, combs...)
- ❏ electrical dryers and razors
- ❏ sterilising
- ❏ hard and soft water
- ❏ hair hygiene (talk from school nurse?)
- ❏ testing shampoos and conditioners

Technology
- ❏ hair coverings (waterproof?)
- ❏ making hair accessories, including beads and flowers
- ❏ tying bows and turbans

History
- ❏ hair styles from different eras – within and beyond living memory

Geography
- ❏ hair styles from a range of cultures

Art
- ❏ copying hair styles
- ❏ designing hair styles
- ❏ combing, brushing, plaiting
- ❏ designing hair accessories

Music
- ❏ creating brushing and cutting sounds
- ❏ listening to and creating hair songs
- ❏ 'Hair' – the song from the musical

Physical education
- ❏ mime cutting hair
- ❏ role play visit to hairdressers or barbers

Religious education
- ❏ hair in the Sikh tradition
- ❏ tying a turban
- ❏ 5 Ks
- ❏ taking Amrit
- ❏ visit to a gurdwara
- ❏ discussion of morality of using animals for shampoo testing

BOOKS
generic but with emphasis on Sikhism

English
- parts of a book
- alphabetical order
- dictionaries
- class books and newspapers
- care of books
- drafting, editing and publishing
- story telling
- library visits
- handwriting and scripts
- fiction and non-fiction

Mathematics
- letter surveys: number of letters on a page
- ordering
- numbering
- Roman numerals
- letter symmetry
- graphs
- book surveys

Science
- types of paper and card
- strengths of paper (wet/dry)
- paper making
- age of trees (growth rings)
- conservation of trees

Technology
- word processing
- printing
- lettering
- book binding
- making books in various formats and styles

History
- Rosetta stone
- Caxton
- ancient books
- hieroglyphics

Geography
- paper
- rain forests

Art
- illuminated manuscripts
- marbling
- book marks
- papier maché
- lettering
- quill pens
- calligraphy
- illustrating stories and designing cover
- images for books

Music
- songs about books
- songs from books
- songs as narrative
- Sikh hymns

Religious education
- holy books: why they are important and how they are used
- stories from scriptures
- the home corner as a base for the Guru Granth Sahib

3. 'FURNISHINGS'

CHANANI

(canopy for Guru Granth Sahib)

Note

This canopy is designed to lay over the cube framework which appears on p.82.

What you need

- 4.8m plain gold silky fabric 120cm wide

- matching thread

- 10m 'fluffy' tinsel

- masking tape

What you do

1. Cut the fabric in half lengthways and join the two halves together by a narrow seam along the selvage to form a square.

2. Turn edges of square approximately 0.5 cm on to the wrong side and turn again. Machine all round.

3. Place canopy over cube and straighten all round so that it falls evenly. On the canopy, mark the corners of the cube and the centre points of each side. Loop tinsel at corners and centre points (as shown in diagram) and catch with tight, neat stitches.

4. When laying finished canopy over cube, hold it in place on the underside with a hinge of masking tape attached to each of the four corners of the cube.

Chanani (using cube framework), with manji sahib, rumala and chaur.

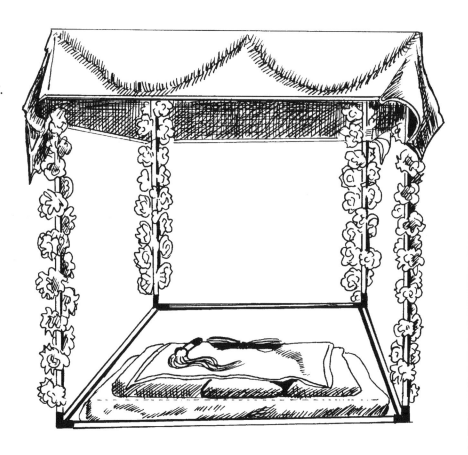

MANJI SAHIB

(cushioned couch for Guru Granth Sahib)

What you need

- foam (old 'camp bed' mattresses will do!) approximately 6cm thick: 1 piece 130cm x 65cm, 2 pieces 50cm x 25cm and 1 piece 45cm x 30cm

- silky, shiny or velvety fabric, plain or with self-pattern, preferably gold in colour: 1 piece 150cm x 150cm, 2 pieces 120cm x 40cm and 1 piece 110cm x 45cm

- matching thread

Note

The fabric need not be new if it is good condition: old velvet curtains, bedspreads or sari lengths are suitable. The three small cushions are a set and should be covered in the same fabric but the larger cushion could be of a different fabric. If different thicknesses of foam are used, adjust sizes of fabric accordingly.

What you do

1. Make all cushions as simple as bags, by folding in half and stitching on three sides. Double-stitching or French seams will add strength.

2. Snip fabric across inside corners and turn bag inside out.

3. Push foam inside bag, turn in open end and slip-stitch to close.

RUMALA

(loose cloths for Guru Granth Sahib)

Note

The large cloth covers the Manji Sahib: on it is placed the Guru Granth Sahib. The two smaller cloths are used to cover the pages of the Guru Granth Sahib, one on each side.

What you need

- 1m x 70cm glittery material in gold colour

- 1m x 70cm silky material in gold colour

- 2 x 50cm x 30cm silky material in gold colour

- 7m gold braid trimming

- matching thread

What you do

1. With wrong sides together, join two large pieces of fabric. Neaten edges and attach braid trim.

2. Neaten edges of smaller pieces and edge with braid trim.

CHAINS OF FLOWERS

(to wind round poles)

What you need

- 80 circles of green tissue, approximately 12cm in diameter
- 80 circles of tissue paper in a variety of colours, approximately 8cm in diameter
- straws (drinking or art) cut into 76 x 7cm lengths
- strong thread
- thick blunt-ended needle

What you do

1. To make each of the four chains of flowers, place a small coloured tissue circle on a green tissue circle and pinch together in the centre to form a flower. Stitch the flower firmly about 20cm from the end of the thread. Thread a length of straw and repeat the flower process. Continue alternating flowers and straws to create a chain of 20 flowers. Cast off, leaving a 20cm length of thread.

2. Bind a chain of flowers loosely round each of the four uprights of the cube framework: use the 20cm lengths of thread to tie the flower chains to the corners of the frame at the top and the bottom.

KACHS

(undershorts)

What you need

- 50cm white polyester/cotton fabric, 1m wide
- 50cm narrow elastic
- white thread

What you do

1. Cut a piece of fabric, 55cm x 50cm.

2. Fold fabric in half along the 50cm edge.

3. To make leg openings, mark the fold and slit open along the fold from 19cm from each end.

4. Face these slits with strips of fabric.

5. Machine the side seams.

6. On wrong side, turn top over 1cm and turn over again. Machine firmly, leaving a small opening to pass elastic.

7. Thread elastic through, adjusting to size required. Secure elastic with strong stitches.

CHAUR

(whisk used when reading Guru Granth Sahib)

What you need

- 20cm length of dowel, approximately 1 cm in diameter

- 10m white/cream macramé string or thick wool

- brown wood stain or renovating shoe polish

- sandpaper

- clear varnish

Close up of Chaur with Guru Granth Sahib

What you do

1. Sand dowel and 'turn' one end if possible.

2. Stain and varnish. Leave to dry until completely hard to the touch.

3. Cut 20 pieces of macramé string each 40cm long.

4. Stick cut lengths onto non-turned end of dowel, approximately 4cm down.

5. Cut a long piece of macramé string and bind cut ends very tightly, finishing with a half-hitch or clove hitch. Coat this securing string thickly with PVA, taking care not to get glue on to loose strings. Leave to dry thoroughly.

6. Lightly brush loose lengths of macramé string to achieve a slightly fluffy effect.

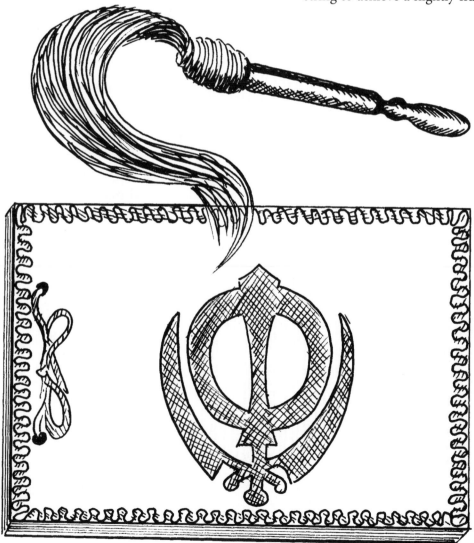

KANGA

(hair comb)

This kanga is for wearing over the neck, as do some Sikhs whose hair has been cut or is not yet long enough. The authentic kanga worn in long hair is flat and made of wood: if this is unobtainable, a fairly realistic alternative is a small, brown, plastic hair comb.

What you need
- kanga template
- thin card
- brown crayon, pencil or felt tip
- if kanga is to be worn round the neck, embroidery thread or thin cord in neutral colour about 40cm long

What you do
1. Photocopy template onto card.
2. Colour brown.
3. Fold over along middle line and stick.
4. Dry flat under a weight.

5. Cut out all round, taking great care between the teeth of the comb.

6. If Kanga is to be worn round neck, use photocopier to reduce the template by half and then follow steps 2 – 5 above. Make a small hole in the middle of the wide band and pass thread or cord through. Adjust to length required and knot firmly.

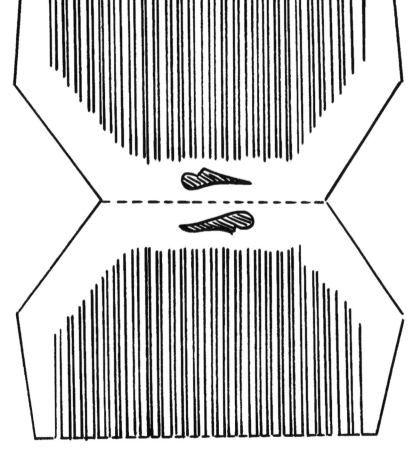

3.5 cm

6 cm

Template for cardboard illustration of adult sized Kanga, with Kirpan motif.

KARA

(bangle)

What you need

- piece of thick card, 0.5cm wide and 10cm long (adjusted to size of child's wrist)
- 3 pieces of thick string – one 30cm, one 20cm and one 10cm long
- small amount of papier maché
- silver spray paint or pens
- masking tape
- PVA

What you do

1. Curl strip of card into circle and join ends firmly with tape.

2. To create raised effect: coat outside of circle with PVA. On outside of circle in the middle of the strip, wrap 30 cm length of string round three times and smooth flat. Coat with PVA. Then wrap 20cm string round twice, pushing string between ridges created by the first three strings. Coat with PVA. Then wrap 10cm string round once, pushing it between ridge created by two strings. Stick with PVA.

3. Apply papier maché thinly to graduate the relief and allow to dry thoroughly

4. Spray or paint silver.

KIRPAN

(symbolic dagger)

What you need
- thick card
- template
- either silver spray paint or pen or aluminium foil and PVA
- 75cm cord or narrow ribbon in neutral colour

What you do

1. Photocopy template and use it to cut out one piece of thick card. Spray or paint silver. If using foil, cut one piece with same template then turn template over and cut a second piece; with PVA, stick foil on to card with the same 'shininess' of foil on both sides of kirpan.

2. Make small hole in handle, pass cord through hole and knot.

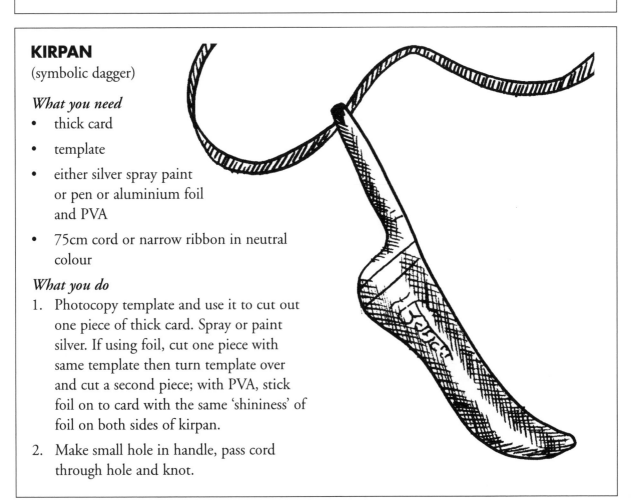

TURBAN

Sikhs are not required to wear a turban but Sikh men with uncut hair universally do so – as do some men whose hair has been cut in the past but who are now growing it. There is some variation in turban styles and tying methods. Boys usually tie a 'patka' – a square of cloth about the size of a handkerchief – over their topknot until they are old enough to keep a turban on. A few women, especially western Sikhs, wear a turban. This child-sized turban is suitable for playing the role of a Sikh man. Young Sikhs may take years to learn to tie their turbans quickly and neatly every morning.

What you need
- 3m x 50cm soft but not slippery fabric (such as lawn or georgette) in any plain colour; if available, a man's turban cut to size to make a manageable length for a child's head
- matching thread
- laundry starch

What you do
1. If the long side is a cut edge, hem it narrowly to avoid fraying. The short edges need not be neatened as they will be tucked in.
2. Starch the fabric, fold it lengthways to form a band about 10cm wide and hang up to dry.

To tie a turban on a child:
1. If the child's hair is long, comb it upwards onto the crown and tie it into a top-knot. Slide a kanga or hair-comb into the back of the top-knot.
2. Sikh men, who usually tie the turban themselves, normally begin by clenching one end of the turban in the teeth to keep it free of the other end and to stop the turban slipping out of control. The child should hold one end securely in front.
3. Wind the turban round the child's head anti-clockwise, covering the ears.
4. With successive windings, spiral the cloth slightly up the head so that the turban covers all but the top-knot.
5. When too little of the turban remains to wind round again, tuck the end into the back of the turban at the top.
6. Open this piece out gently, spread out the top-knot and ease in all round.
7. Release the other piece from the child's grasp, bring it carefully round to the back and over the windings of the turban. Tuck it in at the top.

Opposite: Sequence of combing hair and tying turban

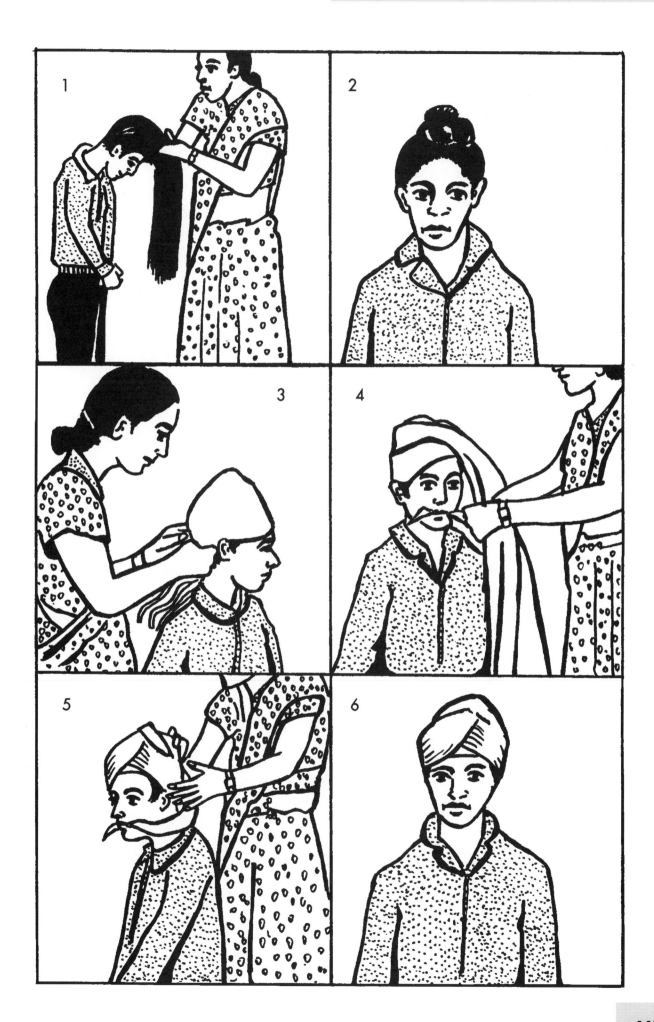

GURU HAAR

(garland featuring picture of Guru)

What you need

- picture of Guru Nanak or Guru Gobind Singh; picture in book can be photocopied
- 50cm 'fluffy' silver or gold tinsel
- 50cm smooth ribbon, about 1cm wide; any colour
- sewing thread in matching colour
- thin white card
- PVA

What you do

1. If using picture in book, photocopy and colour.

2. Cut two pieces of card the same size as the picture of the Guru.

3. Stick picture of Guru on to one piece of card.

4. Attach tinsel all round picture, saving the remainder.

5. Attach both ends of ribbon to back of picture, forming a large loop, as shown.

6. Cut remaining tinsel in two.

7. Using needle and thread and starting at the picture, catch each piece of tinsel to ribbon.

8. Neaten back of picture by gluing second piece of card, covering ends of ribbon and tinsel.

Opposite: Guru Nanak: adult sized haar

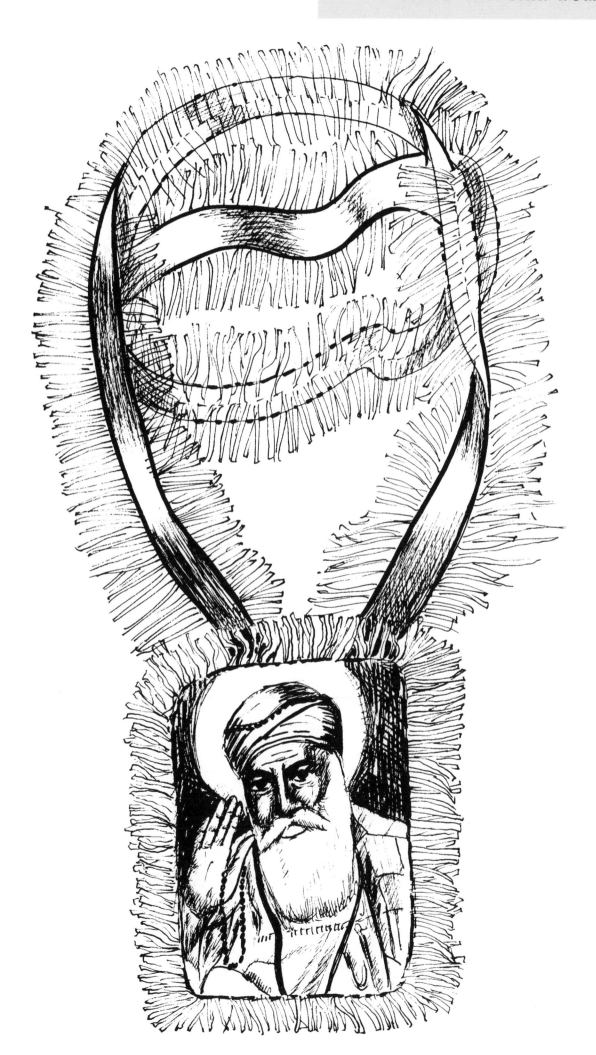

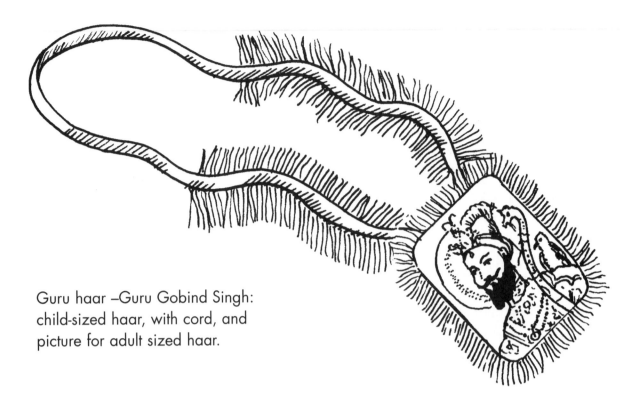

Guru haar –Guru Gobind Singh: child-sized haar, with cord, and picture for adult sized haar.

KURTA, SHALWAR, KAMEEZ AND CHUNI

Suitable clothes for the Sikh 'house' are the **Kurta** (male suit) and **Shalwar**, **Kameez** and **Chuni** (girl's trousers, tunic and long scarf).

Instructions for the **Kurta** are on pages 56-58 and for **Shalwar**, **Kameez** and **Chuni** on pages 116-119.

SHOE RACK

A line drawing and instructions for making the shoe rack are on page 115.

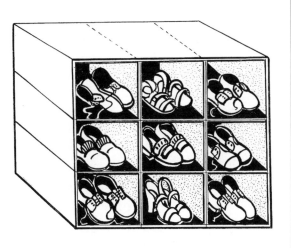

4. FOOD

NAAN BREAD

This flat leavened bread, traditionally cooked in a 'tandoor' oven, is a perfect accompaniment for a savoury dish, whether meat based or vegetarian, and can be served alongside the mash dhal recipe given here.

What you need
- 150ml hot milk (not boiling)
- 2 teaspoons castor sugar
- 2 teaspoons dried yeast
- 450g plain flour
- teaspoon salt
- 1 teaspoon baking powder
- 2 teaspoons vegetable oil
- 150ml plain, beaten yogurt
- 1 large egg
- cling film

What you do
1. Pour the milk into a bowl. Add the yeast and 1 teaspoon of sugar. Mix thoroughly and leave for 20 minutes until the mixture is frothy.

2. Sift the flour, salt and baking powder into a large bowl. Add the rest of the sugar, the milk mixture, the oil, yogurt and egg. Mix together and form into a ball of dough.

3. On a clean surface, knead the dough for about 10 minutes and form into a ball.

4. Roll in a little oil, and put into a bowl, covering it with cling film. Leave to rise for 1 hour.

5. Preheat the oven to the highest temperature and put in a heavy baking tray. Preheat the grill.

6. Knead the dough and divide into 6 balls. Shape each ball into a tear-shaped naan bread.

7. Put the naan on to the baking tray and cook for 3 minutes.

8. When the naan has puffed up, grill it for 30 seconds and then wrap in a clean cloth.

9. Repeat for all the balls of dough and serve hot.

KARAH PRASHAD

This is a sweet and sticky dish, made and distributed on religious occasions. While it is being made, prayers are said; when the prayers are over, the dish is ready to be given to all those present. A small amount of the mixture is placed in the hands of those who wish to partake, and is eaten with the fingers.

Note
If the dish is not being made for a religious occasion, but as a dessert dish, any of the following flavours can be added: rose water, sweet spices and almonds.

What you need
- 110g of unsalted butter
- 50g atta (chapati flour) or plain flour
- 110g semolina
- 400ml water
- 110g sugar

Note
Keep the heat low throughout.

What you do
1. Combine the water and sugar and bring to the boil.

2. Melt the butter in a saucepan, add the flour and beat well with a wooden spoon.

3. Pour in the semolina and beat well. Heat until the butter separates.

4. Gradually add the sugared water and beat until a paste is formed. If the mixture gets too firm, add more butter.

MASH DHAL

This is a savoury vegetable dish. Although some Sikhs eat meat (except for beef), many are vegetarian. Vegetarian food is always served at the langar (the 'free kitchen' in a gurdwara) and at Sikh functions so that everyone may eat.

Sikhs use black lentils for dhal: they take longer to cook than red lentils and so absorb the spices more fully, improving the flavour. In the north of India, the food is far milder than in the south, where spices are added to preserve the food in the hot climate.

You will need

- 225g black lentils
- 1 litre water
- vegetable oil
- 2 fresh green finely chopped chillies
- 450g chopped onions
- 2 cloves of garlic, peeled and crushed
- 4 fresh tomatoes, pureed
- 2 tablespoons of tomato puree
- a chunk of fresh ginger (about the size of a walnut)
- 50g butter or cream (optional)
- spinach or very small florets of cauliflower (optional)

Note

The onion, garlic and ginger should be as fine as possible: they may be liquidised.

What you do

1. Boil the lentils in the water.
2. Heat the oil in a frying pan and fry the onion, garlic, chillies and ginger until browned.
3. Add the tomatoes and tomato puree. If using cauliflower or spinach, add now.
4. Stir this mixture into the black dhal and water.
5. Simmer for 1-2 hours. The longer this dish is allowed to cook the better but keep an eye on the water level.
6. Add the butter or cream, if used, just before serving and stir thoroughly.
7. Serve with rice and a green salad.

5. BOOKS

(simplified and paraphrased extracts from the
Guru Granth Sahib)

There is one God.
He is the Truth.
He made everything.
He is not afraid.
He loves everyone.
He is everywhere.
He is not born.
He does not die.
He helps you to love him.
He is the Truth.
He was the Truth.
He always will be the Truth.

You are the ocean. I am a little fish. Wherever
I am, you are there. Without you, I would die.

You are the tree. Your beautiful branches are
everywhere.

You are the ocean, the foam and the bubbles.
Everything that I can see is you.

You are the string and the jewels. You are the
knot that ties the necklace together.

I am like a little frog. I only know what
happens in my own pond. By loving you, I
can see all that you can see, and know all that
you know.

I am an elephant, wandering lost in the forest.
You will help me find my way home.

You are very dear to me, as dear as milk is to
the baby, as the flower is the humming bee, as
the pond is to the fish. As I need water on a
hot day, I need you.

I love you, and I am as happy as the lotus
blossom floating upon the water.

The way I look, the clothes I wear, the things I
have, these are not important if I do not have
you.

The Khanda symbol which may be used
on the cover of the Guru Granth Sahib.

Beautiful palaces, shining and bright, will not
be happy places without you.

If I am kind to everyone, even when they are
unkind to me, I will make you happy and I
will be happy too.

I am as small as a trickling stream. By loving
you, I will become as strong as a river.

I do not need to look for you in wild and
faraway places for you are always in my
heart, and everywhere around me.

I am like a little boat, tossed into the stormy
sea. Catch me in your fisherman's net and
bring me safely to the shore.

Who made the stars
That twinkle in the midnight sky?
Who made the sun?
Who made the moon?
Whose light is all around me?
Who makes the waves rise up from the sea?
Who makes the seeds sprout and grow?
Who ripens the fruit on the trees?

BIBLIOGRAPHY

INFORMATION FOR ADULTS AND OLDER CHILDREN, INCLUDING GUIDANCE FOR TEACHERS

Alan Brown, John Rankin and Angela Wood, *Religions*, Longman.

Deirdre Burke, *Food and Fasting* (Understanding Religions), Wayland.

Anita Compton, *Marriage Customs* (Understanding Religions), Wayland.

Paul Gateshill and Jan Thompson, *Religious Artefacts in the Classroom – a practical guide for primary and secondary teachers*, Hodder and Stoughton.

Lucy Rushton, *Birth Customs* (Understanding Religions), Wayland.

Lucy Rushton, *Death Customs* (Understanding Religions), Wayland.

Christianity
John Logan, *Christianity* (World Religions), Wayland.

Maurice Lynch, *Easter*, BFSS National RE Centre.

Jan Thompson, *The Christian Faith and its Symbols*, Hodder & Stoughton.

Hinduism
Dilip Kadodwala, *Hinduism* (World Religions), Wayland.

V. P. (Hemant) Kanitkar, *Hindu Scriptures*, Heinemann

Jenny Rose, *Hindu Story and Symbol*, BFSS National RE Centre.

Islam
Khadijah Knight, *Islam* (World Religions), Wayland.

R. Maqsood, *The Qur'an*, Heinemann.

Jenny Rose, *Islamic Story, Folklore and Pattern*, BFSS National RE Centre

The Prophets, IQRA Trust.

Judaism
Douglas Charing, *The Torah*, Heinemann.

Angela Wood, *Judaism* (World Religions), Wayland.

Angela Wood, *Jewish Festivals*, Heinemann.

Sikhism
Kanwaljit Kaur-Singh, *Sikhism* (World Religions), Wayland.

Kanwaljit Kaur-Singh, *Sikh Festivals*, Heinemann.

Piara Singh Sambhi, *Guru Granth Sahib*, Heinemann.

BOOKS FOR CHILDREN

Christianity
Margaret Barratt, *An Egg for Babcha* (Bridges to Religions – The Warwick RE Project), Heinemann.

Margaret Barratt, *Lucy's Sunday* (Bridges to Religions – The Warwick RE Project), Heinemann.

Margaret Killingray, *I am an Anglican*, Franklin Watts.

Brenda Pettenuzzo, *I am a Pentecostal*, Franklin Watts.

Brenda Pettnuzzo, *I am a Roman Catholic*, Franklin Watts.

Maria Roussou, *I am a Greek Orthodox*, Franklin Watts.

Jan Thompson, *Christian Festivals (Celebrate)*, Heinemann.

Carol Watson, *Christian (Beliefs and Cultures)*, Watts.

Hinduism
Manju Aggarawal, *I am a Hindu*, Franklin Watts.

Ruskin Bond, *The Adventures of Rama and Sita*, Walker Books.

C. Deshpande, *Diwali*, A & C Black.

Anita Ganeri, *Hindu (Beliefs and Cultures)*, Watts.

Anita Ganeri, *What Do We Know About Hinduism?*, Macdonald Young Books.

Madhu Jaffrey, *Seasons of Splendour*, Puffin.

Dilip Kadodwala and Paul Gateshill, *Hindu Festivals (Celebrate)*, Heinemann.

Pratima Mitchell, *The Ramayana*, Puffin.

Dilip Kadodwala, *My Hindu Life* (Everyday Religion), Wayland.

Islam
Margaret Barratt, *Something to Share* (Bridges to Religions – The Warwick RE Project), Heinemann.

Riadh El-Droubie, *My Muslim Life* (Everyday Religion), Wayland.

Shahrukh Husein, *What Do We Know About Islam?*, MacDonald Young Books.

M. S. Kayani, *A Great Friend of Children*, The Islamic Foundation.

Cristina Kessler, *Muhammad's Desert Night*, Victor Gollancz.

Khadijah Knight, *Islamic Festivals (Celebrate)*, Heinemann.

Mustafa Yusuf McDermott, *Muslim Nursery Rhymes*, The Islamic Foundation.

Khurram Murad, *Assalamu Alaikum – peace be with you*, The Islamic Foundation.

Khurram Murad, *Love at Home*, The Islamic Foundation.

Abu Bakar Nazir, *I am a Muslim*, Franklin Watts.

Richard Tames, *Muslim (Beliefs and Cultures)*, Watts.

Judaism
Margaret Barratt, *The Seventh Day is Shabbat* (Bridges to Religions – The Warwick RE Project), Heinemann.

Anne Clarke and David Rose, *My Jewish Life (Everyday Religion)*, Wayland.

Doreen Fine, *What Do We Know About Judaism?*, Macdonald Young Books.

Clive Lawton, *I am a Jew*, Franklin Watts.

S. Oberman & T. Lewin, *Always Adam*, Gollancz Paperbacks.

Eric Ray, *Sofer – The Story of a Torah Scroll*, Torah Aura Publications.

Monica Stoppleman, *Jewish (Beliefs and Cultures)*, Watts.

Angela Wood, *Jewish Festivals (Celebrate)*, Heinemann.

Angela Wood, *Passover*, Wayland.

Sikhism
Manju Aggarwal, *I am a Sikh*, Franklin Watts.

Catherine Chambers, *Sikh (Beliefs and Cultures)*, Watts.

John Coutts, *Sikh Festivals (Celebrate)*, Heinemann.

Beryl Dhanjal, *What Do We Know About Sikhism?*, Macdonald Young Books.

Kanwaljit Kaur-Singh, *My Sikh Life (Everyday Religion)*, Wayland.

USEFUL ADDRESSES

The following contact details are correct at the time of going to print.

Bharatiya Vidya Bhavan
(Institute of Indian Culture)
4A Castledown Road
London W14
0171 381 3086
A wide-ranging cultural programme, including dance and music classes, performances and concerts, and public lectures; advice and information about Indian culture, especially the Hindu tradition

BFSS National RE Centre
Brunel University
Osterley Campus
Borough Road
Isleworth
Middlesex TW7 5DU
Tel: 0181 891 0121 Ext.: 2658
Publications and in-service training

Board of Deputies of British Jews
Education Dept
Woburn House
Tavistock Square
London WC1H 0EZ
Tel: 0171 543 5400
Information on Jewish resources, visits and visitors to schools

Centre for Jewish Education
80 East End Road
Finchley
London N3 2SY
Tel: 0181 349 9484
Resources, information and advice about teaching Judaism

Christian Aid
Inter-Church House
35 – 41 Lower Marsh
London SE1 7RL
Tel: 0171 620 4444
A wide variety of resources and advice on the work of aid agencies

Christian Education
Movement
Royal Buildings
Victoria Street
Derby DE1 1GW
Tel: 01332 296655
Termly mailings of RE Today, REsource, Look, Hear! and British Journal of Religious Education, as well as other teaching resources.

Gohil Emporium
381 Stratford Pond
Sparkhill
Birmingham
B11 4JZ
Tel: 0121 771 3048
Artefacts from India

The Inter Faith Network
5 – 7 Tavistock Place
London WC1H 9SS
Tel: 0171 388 0008
A national body of inter-faith groups, many of which focus on education; holds contact list of national religious bodies

IQRA Trust
24 Culross Street
London W1Y 3HE
Tel: 0171 491 1572
Publications and advice on teaching Islam

Islamic Book Centre
120 Drummond Street
London NW1E 2HL
Tel: 0171 388 0710
Islamic books and artefacts

The Islamic Foundation
Markfield Dawah Centre
Ratby Lane
Markfield
Leicester LE6 0RN
Tel: 01530 244944/5
Resources for teaching Islam

Islamic Cultural Centre
Park Road
London NW8
Tel: 0171 724 3363
Information on Islam; extensive library with titles in Arabic, English and some other languages

ISKCON Education Service
Bhaktivedanta Manor
Letchmore Heath
Watford
Herts WD2 8EP
Tel: 01923 859578
Information on, and advice about teaching, Hinduism and Krishna Consciousness; courses and visits for pupils and teachers

Jewish Education Bureau
8 Westcombe Avenue
Leeds LS8 1BS
Tel: 01532 663613
Jewish books, leaflets and artefacts; advice on teaching Judaism

Jewish Memorial Council
Bookshop
25 Enford Street
London W1
Tel: 0171 724 7778
Jewish books and artefacts; mail order and personal shoppers

Manor House Books
80 East End Road
Finchley
London N3 2SY
Tel: 0181 349 9484
Jewish resources and books; mail order and personal shoppers

The National Society RE Centre
36 Causton Street
London SW1P 4AU
Tel: 0171 932 1190
Publications and a resource library; Church of England foundation but offering resources from many faiths

Pictorial Charts Educational Trust
17 Kirchen Road
London W13 0UD
Tel: 0181 567 9206
Posters and picture packs by mail order

The Regional RE Centre (Midlands)
Westhill College
Weoley Park Road
Selly Oak
Birmingham B29 6LL
Tel: 0121 472 7245 Ext.: 258
Resources (some produced at the centre), courses and visits for teachers

Shap Working Party on World Religions in Education
c/o The National Society (above)
Annual journal and annotated calendar of festivals; information and advice for teachers

Sikh Council For Interfaith Relations
43 Dorset Road
Merton Park
London SW19 3EZ
0181 540 4148
Information and advice

Sikh Missionary Sociey (UK)
10 Featherstone Road
Southall
Middlesex UB2 5AA
0181 574 1902
Information and advice; publications and lectures

INDEX OF ARTEFACTS

'Furnishings', 'Food' and 'Books'

HINDU

JEWISH

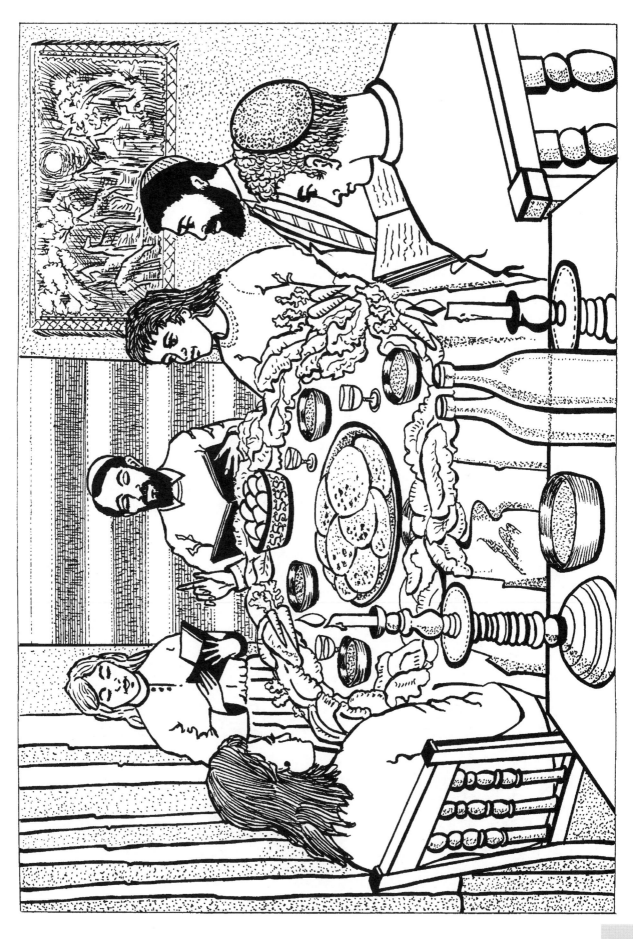

MUSLIM

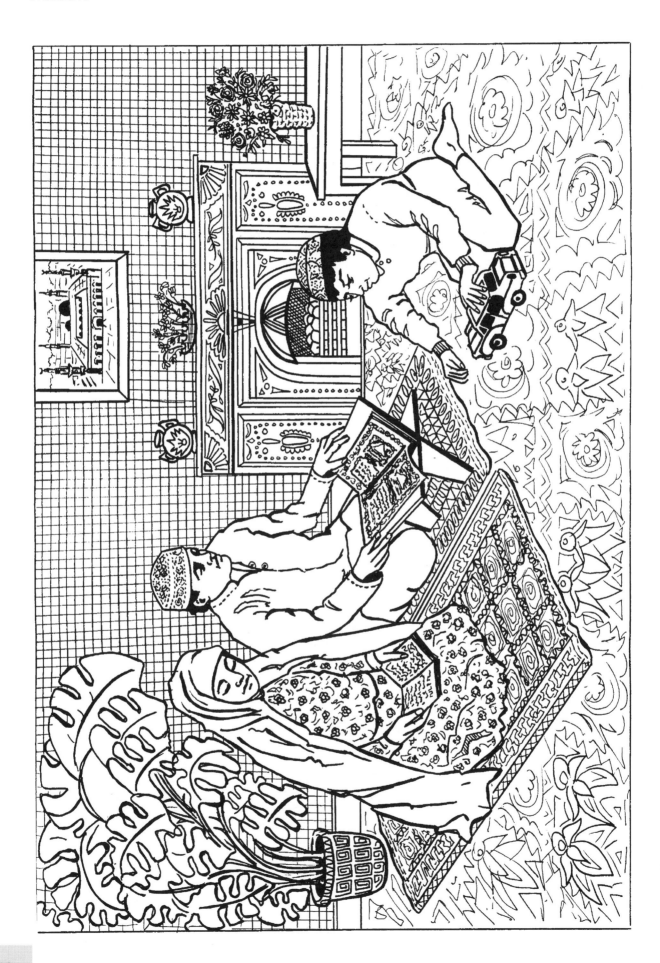

SIKH

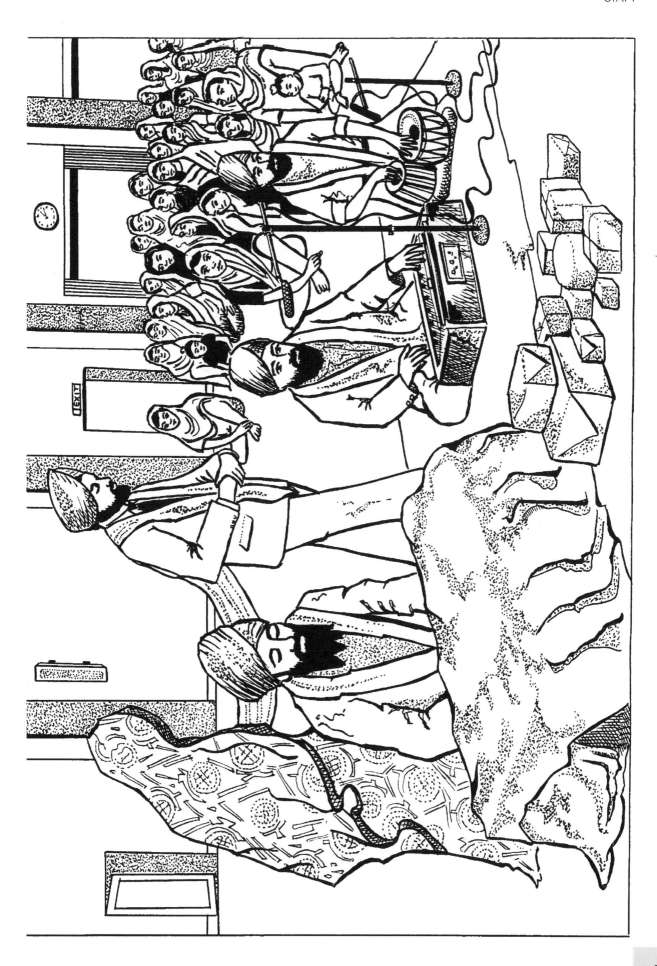